MW00442287

PRAISE
THE DIRTY SIDE OF LEADERSHIP

As a 20 year "survivor" of leadership positions in both the private and government sectors, I wish this book was available when I first began my leadership journey, it certainly would have saved me some time, energy and heartache. As any good leader knows, there certainly is a "dirty side" to leadership. The Dirty Lessons integrated throughout the book are priceless and on point as they relate to leadership. Ron has hit a home run with *The Dirty Side of Leadership*.

— GREG FOREST
Retired Chief U.S. Probation and Pretrial Services Officer

Ron is a leader in government that everyone can learn from. His personal stories and experiences can benefit anyone. *The Dirty Side of Leadership* is a must read for those who lead and supervise others.

— JAMES GREGORIUS
Associate Director for Operations,
Federal Law Enforcement Training Centers, Retired

In my life of trying to improve in my leadership of others, I have often picked up the latest book on leadership. It was my hope to find a nice simple plan that I could implement. Something that would keep the messiness away, eliminate the mistakes, smooth over the bumps. What I often find are books filled with philosophy and strategy but very little practicality and authenticity. Ron's book is real. It is written from a real leader's perspective. He doesn't pretend to wow you with all the great things he has done but he's more interested in being honest. I love his authenticity of sharing real stories of ups and downs. You won't find this in a typical leadership book. All successful leaders have to navigate the dirty side from time to time. I encourage you to allow Ron to help you navigate yours!

— TIM RIDDLE
CEO, Discover Blind Spots LLC

Ron Ward is a relational and authentic leader, no matter the setting or audience. I've worked with Ron on various team-development initiatives over the past 25 years. and I've witnessed his leadership and management which has been driven with an individual focus and all-inclusive impact! As a 20-year-veteran of student development in higher education, and long-time advisor and emotional intelligence coach for Millennial and Generation Z leaders, the Dirty Side of Leadership is a must-read for emerging leaders working to affect healthy and lasting change!

— STEVE GALLAGHER
Founder, IDEATE Coaching & Consulting,
Executive Director of Student Affairs,
University of North Carolina School of the Arts

Chief Ward takes you on a leadership journey from start to finish. There are so many lessons and take aways, not only for the current or new manager, but for those individuals looking to lead. One walks away from this book with the knowledge that leadership and learning lessons are on every road traveled.

— CRAIG PENET
President of the Federal Probation
and Pretrial Officers Association

In the Dirty Side of Leadership, Ron provides intimate details into his life and the early years of his career, while depicting the growth into a leadership role. Using his intelligence and dedication to his career in Federal law enforcement and management, along with his ability to convey the dirty lessons within the scope of the story, allows the reader to experience the process that is necessary to be a successful manager. Fantastic experience and delivery of knowledge to become an effective manager that was also very entertaining.

— KIMBERLY TRIPLETT
DO, Medical Director

I have known Ron Ward both personally and professionally for the past 12 years and cannot think of anyone who, as Academy Director, has done more to advance the cause of wellness throughout the U.S. Probation and Pretrial Services system. As a person and leader who has been tried and tested in both his personal and professional life, Ron's ability to persevere through the many challenges undoubtedly comes from the holistic approach he takes to leadership. In the Dirty Side of Leadership, Ron conveys his unwavering passion and commitment to serve others and provides the anecdote for leaders to thrive, not just survive, every facet of their lives. Ron's presentation style and powerful message is effective and appeals to all audiences.

— RICH ELIAS
Founder, Rich Elias Consulting – LLC

Most leadership books are a waste of time, portraying strategies with irrepressible optimism that all bad employees can be turned good, all problems are opportunities for better times, and being a boss can be all fun and games. The truth is being a boss is not always a day at a sunny beach, sometimes it is gut wrenchingly hard. *The Dirty Side of Leadership* is the book that finally details ways leaders can prepare for, as well as respond to, the most difficult times all decision makers will eventually face. A fun treat to read, this book is a highly rewarding experience for both new and experienced leaders.

— DOUG BURRIS
Retired Chief U.S. Probation Officer
and subject of the 2016 movie *Out of the Box*

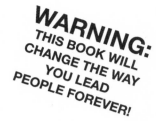

WARNING:
THIS BOOK WILL
CHANGE THE WAY
YOU LEAD
PEOPLE FOREVER!

THE DIRTY SIDE OF
LEADERSHIP

From the Appalachian Coalfields to a rise in Federal
Law Enforcement: A Leadership Journey

BY RON WARD

Palmetto Publishing Group
Charleston, SC

The Dirty Side of Leadership
Copyright © 2020 by Ron Ward
All rights reserved

All rights reserved. No part of this book may be reproduced or transmitted in any form or by any means, electronic or mechanical, including photocopying, recording, or by any information storage and retrieval system without written permission from the author, except for the inclusion of quotations in a review.

This book is only for educational purposes. The views expressed are those of the author alone. The reader is responsible for his or her own actions. Adherence to all applicable laws and regulations, including international, federal, state, and local laws governing professional licensing, business practices, advertising, and all other aspects of doing business in the United States, Canada, or any other jurisdiction is the sole responsibility of the purchaser or reader. Neither the author nor the publisher assumes any responsibility or liability whatsoever on behalf of the purchaser or reader of these materials.

This is a work of nonfiction. Nonetheless, some of the names, personal characteristics, and, in some instances, conduct, have been changed or modified to protect identities. Any resulting resemblances to persons living or dead is entirely coincidental and unintentional.

First Edition

Printed in the United States

ISBN-13: 978-1-64111-743-2
ISBN-10: 1-64111-743-5

DEDICATION

This book is dedicated to my wonderful parents, Joe and Doris Ward. Thank you for the love and support you have given me throughout my life. Most of all thank you for teaching me the power of serving others.

To my daughters, Haley Ridley and Jansen Ward, my son-in-law, Stephen Ridley, and my new grandson, Nathan Archer Ridley. You are my world.

TABLE OF CONTENTS

Author's Note: Part of this book was written during the Covid-19 pandemic. Nonetheless, the principles contained herein can still be applied.

FOREWORD

On October 14th, 1912, Theodore Roosevelt was scheduled to deliver an exhilarating speech to a crowd in Milwaukee. Thousands gathered in front of the Gilpatrick Hotel to support his election for a Third Term as President of the United States.

As Roosevelt approached the podium, the saloonkeeper John Schrank pulled out his gun, aimed for the heart and fired a .32-caliber bullet into Roosevelt's chest.

Were it not for the glasses case and crumpled speech papers in his coat pocket, the shot would have likely killed Roosevelt. Despite bullet fragments in his chest, Roosevelt stepped onstage and delivered the speech as scheduled.

After his introduction, the former President pulled out the bloody papers from his jacket pocket and exclaimed, "You see, it takes more than one bullet to kill a Bull Moose."

He spoke for almost an hour and then rushed to the hospital.

At times, leadership can be dirty. Shot in the chest kind of dirty.

Unlike how it is typically depicted, leadership is hardly ever smooth sailing.

I first met Ron more than a decade ago. Over the years, we've swapped countless stories about the leadership challenges we faced.

Most leadership training focuses on how to lead when things are going well, but neglects to equip people for difficult situations. In order to become a great leader, we must learn to be comfortable with the uncomfortable.

In his book, Ron shares powerful, firsthand accounts to help us navigate the dirty side of leadership. He provides practical guidance on how to act when things don't go as planned and tough situations arise. It is both action-oriented and engaging. Simply put, I wish I had this book when I started out as an entrepreneur.

Now, more than ever, the world needs effective leaders. Whether at home with our children or with colleagues in the workplace, we all lead in various ways.

Ron's lessons are just as applicable in those environments as they are in government service.

This book can serve as your guide to help you develop into a better leader, wherever you are. It may even help you dodge some bullets.

Get ready - you're in for a real treat.

JUSTIN L. FULCHER
Founder and former CEO of RingMD
August 2020

PREFACE

I'm lying in bed; my mind is racing. I just can't get comfortable. I look at my phone—midnight. If ever I've needed a good night's sleep, it's tonight. At 9:30 tomorrow morning, I have to terminate a tenured employee who falsified timesheets. It's my job to drop the anvil. Lucky me. I turn on the light and try to read with little success, then I try again. Finally, I fall asleep around 2:00 a.m. After what seems like fifteen minutes, the alarm goes off.

Ugh! I hate that sound.

It's 5:30 a.m. I get up, shower, make my health shake, drink some coffee. Put on one of my best suits—have to dress the part.

Morning commute. Arrive at my office at 7:15 a.m.

And wait.

Finally, 9:00 a.m. I'm exhausted—the kind of exhaustion where it takes too much energy to even determine how I feel. Thirty minutes and counting.

It had taken me and two other managers numerous hours over three days to connect the dots. In matters like these, a specific itinerary must be in place that includes sharing the investigation with senior management, seeking guidance from the internal legal office, conducting a conference with human resources, and arranging for a security officer to be in the office next to mine—you can't be too careful in today's world.

The emergency signal is in place to notify security in case things turn ugly. Security officials are on standby, also waiting for him to arrive. There are cardboard boxes hidden in the adjacent office waiting for him so that he can collect his personal belongings and, hopefully, expedite his exit from the premises.

Tick-tock. The clock in my office reminds me how slowly seconds can pass in times like these. Every minute that passes feels like a minor panic attack.

My mind is racing. I feel a tension headache coming on. I'm not sure if Tylenol or a morphine drip would better serve me. I try to remember strategies from the superfluous motivational/leadership books I've read over the years, as if by the grace of God, some lightning bolt of pliable information will magically surface from the depths of my brain. But it would seem that, credible though they are, those books didn't provide me with the direction and courage I need to muster by 9:30 a.m.

Then it starts: The self-doubt creeps in like a crazy ex-girlfriend who just discovered my new cell number. I start to question myself and my conduct over the years: Had I ever lied? Or bent the rules? I mean, I'm no saint, and I'm about to alter the course of this guy's life—his future, his family's future.

I become acutely aware of the lump in the back of my throat. My mouth feels as dry as the Sahara Desert. It becomes hard to swallow.

At first, my big promotion looked sexy. The big office, the chance to influence the agency, travel, a generous pay raise. What's not to love? But now, none of that seems to matter.

It's 9:10. I skim through my notes one last time. I feel my heart beating; my hands are slightly trembling like the day after a night of binge-drinking.

I receive word that he has arrived and is sitting in his car. Waiting.

What must he be thinking right now? Will he admit his conduct? Will he think I'm the biggest prick on the planet? What if he appeals, forcing management into a long, drawn out cat and mouse game? No.

We need this to end quickly so we can backfill his position. We are short-staffed as it is. *Please God.*

Hopefully it will be over in just a few minutes. After all, what are a few minutes compared to an entire lifetime?

Okay, Ron, focus. You've got this. I knew at some point I would have to do something like this—I just didn't think it would be this soon.

Okay. 9:20 a.m. *Deep breath.* I conference in HR and ask another manager to be present as a witness.

Tap-tap-tap. A brisk knock on the door.

Showtime.

ACKNOWLEDGMENTS

My sincere gratitude to my wonderful parents, Joe and Doris Ward. Dad, your concern for others and your work ethic is inspiring. Mom, your kindness is like nonother.

Thank you to my daughters, Haley Ridley and Jansen Ward, my son-in-law, Stephen Ridley, and my new grandson, Nathan Archer Ridley. Thank you for tolerating me when I continually talked about the challenges of writing this book. You all will change the world for the better.

To my sister, Becky Cook and Brother-in-law, Mark Cook. Your love for others is contagious!

I want to express my gratitude to Director James C. Duff and Deputy Director Lee Ann Bennett of the Administrative Office of the US Courts. It was an honor to serve with you. Your leadership, particularly during the Covid-19 Pandemic, was unsurpassed. You help make the Judiciary the best Branch of the federal government.

Special thanks to those who attempted to manage me, both past and present, at the Office of Probation and Pretrial Services. John Hughes, Matthew Rowland, John Fitzgerald, Nancy Beatty and Charles Robinson. You provided me with so many great opportunities and each of you enhanced my quest to become a better leader. We had a tremendous journey.

To my fellow Federal Law Enforcement Training Accreditation board members and the Office of Accreditation. You are government at its best.

Thank you to staff, both past and present, of the Federal Probation and Pretrial Academy, and, particularly, Branch Chiefs, Gene DiMaria, Mary Jean Gagnon-Odom, Cynthia Mazzei and Stephanie Denton. Thank you for your dedication to training and for always covering my blind spots.

There were several people who provided guidance and inspiration along this journey. Your encouragement and knowledge kept this pursuit alive:

Justin Fulcher, Sabastian Marshall, Lisa Muggeo, Erin Miller, Steve Gallagher, Julie Och, Carrie Kent, Danny Kuhn, Hannah Drake, Cindy Caltagirone, Jeff Curtis and Mark Ryan.

To my mentors, Dr. Sam Samples, Dr. Ron Crum and Dave Stevens. Thank you for investing in me.

Special thanks to Michelle Paradis for your long hours of edits and late-night pep talks.

Grateful to God for my life and my Lord and Savior, Jesus Christ, for the ultimate sacrifice.

THE MANAGERS CREED

Leadership challenge – Read two times per day for thirty days.

I am a leader. I strive to serve the staff for whom I am responsible, and through this service, together we enhance every part of our organization.

First and foremost, I am a leader of people. I operate with integrity and strive to be the best I can be. Through my efforts, I help all employees to reach their full potential. I will not settle for mediocrity but strive for excellence.

I balance my work and personal life to keep myself fresh and prepared for the position I hold. I am a lifelong learner and will continue this journey throughout my career.

When I make mistakes, I take responsibility and work to improve.

When I have victories, I share the credit.

I communicate in clear and straightforward terms and seek input from my superiors and staff to promote a professional workplace where everyone is valued and respected.

I regularly interact with staff to make sure they are getting what they need from me.

I arrive each day with a plan to win, no matter what lies before me.

I have the courage to take on negative behaviors, confront bullies, and challenge negative circumstances.

I strive to win, for I am a leader, a leader who produces champions!

INTRODUCTION

I was speaking to about 150 senior managers and I started with a question: Raise your hand if you have dealt with a personnel issue over the past thirty days. Nearly all hands went up.

The past two weeks?

About half of the hands went up.

This week?

About a third of the hands went up.

This morning during this conference? Five hands went up.

It didn't surprise me. Here's the deal: People are unpredictable and managing the unpredictable is flippin' hard.

Management includes some tough stuff—confronting poor performance, standing up against bullies, terminating employees, having stern communication with stakeholders, and making life-changing decisions.

Most management training doesn't cover these "dirtier" issues that often. But even when it does, it almost never covers how to *become* the type of manager and leader that has the courage and skills to perform under pressure. Theory might be useful, but at the end of the day, you've got to be able to put it into practice.

I want to do something unique with this book.

My job has meant overseeing the training of thousands of people in use-of-force decision making, firearms, edged-weapon defensive,

defensive tactics, and many other instructional courses. What I am most proud of, however, is teaching people to promote dignity and respect and to have a positive impact on the lives of others.

Outside of my career, I've also worked with dozens of people hands-on who were coming into management and leadership positions, both formally and informally. There have been roles in church and social organizations, there have been law enforcement roles, there have been all sorts of casual interactions with people in everything from large multinational corporations to small family-run local businesses.

There's a place for all different types of leadership and mentorship. But one of the most important ones is rarely talked about in books and that is:

Raw honesty during informal, personal mentorship.

Table talk.

There are all kinds of books on policies and procedures, all kinds of instruction that ranges from basic skills to advanced algorithms. You can go get a bachelor's or master's degree and learn the fundamentals, and touch on intermediate and advanced topics.

But how things really get done tends to be a one-on-one thing. Over coffee, tea, drinks, food.

I want you to see me as a mentor, or your personal coach. We get together a few times a month for coffee, in person or virtually, and talk about the real stuff. The stuff that's usually left out of mainstream management bestsellers.

During these intimate chats, we look behind the veil of leadership and talk about some areas that are not often discussed in books and training programs.

Most leadership materials are very impersonal. But to be a leader, you've got to draw inspiration and lessons from everything that's happened in your life.

I'll give you my beginnings, no BS, from a world that pretty much doesn't exist anymore. This will include Coal Country. Deputy sheriff. All this before Wi-Fi and GPS and smart phones. It was a different world. Sometimes rough. Sometimes exciting. Sometimes desperate.

My stories will look different than yours, but I want you to understand where I started picking up the lessons of life and help you to identify those in yourself. I'll share funny moments, but also stories about getting bullied or dealing with crazy situations, including tragedy. You've got those stories too.

You need to learn from them.

Not my stories. Your own. You need to understand them and incorporate them. They're already who you are.

I learned a lot about human nature from the twists and turns that led to my career in law enforcement, my progression as a police officer, a U.S. probation officer, instructor, and rising to become an academy director/division chief at a federal law enforcement academy.

Your path is going to be different than mine. But you've had a path. Use it. I'll help.

There were times when I felt alone and had many sleepless nights, but I share with you that I believe with the proper support and realistic solutions, much of my stress could have been lessened, and I could have avoided many of the pitfalls that I experienced.

After we finish a lot of coffee and talk about life and leadership, I believe we will grow and learn together along this journey.

So, however you take your coffee—Iced? Black? Sugar? —sit down and get comfortable. But not too comfortable.

Let's get started.

PART I

THE JOURNEY

In order to understand someone, you must understand their journey.

Some of the stories I'm going to share are funny. Some are interesting. But some are painful. Some of the memories are painful to this day.

Leadership isn't always an obvious path, and most leaders have stories like mine. Different, of course. But the same types of things. You do too.

I want to help you understand how I got here, the sometimes crazy twists in the path from a young boy in Coal Country to running a federal academy to becoming chair of a prestigious federal law enforcement board. I learned a lot about people, about life, about leading.

There will be 100 dirty lessons (DL) for short placed strategically throughout this writing for you to ponder.

One more sip of coffee. Let's do this.

CHAPTER 1: EARLY CHILDHOOD

COAL COUNTRY

I grew up in the coalfields of southwestern Virginia. Population at that time was approximately 500. It wasn't exactly a thriving metropolis. As a matter of fact, there was one locally owned store, a restaurant, a post office, and one school for K-12. My graduating class was thirty-nine kids which made it easier to make the top ten. I had friends nicknamed Turkey, Chicken, Butter, and Dough Boy. Our favorite mode of transportation was the back of a pickup truck. Broken English was the language of the land, so I struggled with some adaptation later in life.

Heck, I was nine years old before I had my first bite of McDonald's. My parents drove nearly two hours into Tennessee for a doctor's appointment with the promise that we would stop at McDonald's on the way back home. I had seen Ronald McDonald in commercials and was sure that he would be there to greet me, but he must have been on a lunch break.

I didn't let that get my nine-year-old self down. I ordered a hamburger and within minutes, it arrived. I didn't even have to sit down and wait.

However, things were about to take a nose-dive like a WWII plane shot down by the enemy. I went to a booth with my parents, opened the burger, and took a quick bite. To my utter shock, something was wrong—terribly wrong. I opened the burger and realized it only had mustard, ketchup, and pickles. Who eats a hamburger without tomato and mayonnaise?! No, seriously!

I was so upset that my parents ordered me a Big Mac in a desperate attempt to calm me down. I took a bite of that scrumptious delight, and it must have been the special sauce. I loved it. All was right with the world again.

DL #1: If you don't have a Plan B, C, and D, Plan A may leave you in a lurch. Solid managers build a web of alternate plans.

HIGH WATER

I spent most of my summers barefoot. Putting on shoes was an unnecessary waste of time. Can you imagine? But hold off on the banjo music. While there were many humorous things about the coalfields, including areas such as Chicken Ridge, Bear Wallow, Harry's Branch, and Pea Patch—I couldn't make these names up if I tried—there were also hardships and tragedy.

It was somewhat routine to hear that a coal miner had been fatally crushed after the top had collapsed inside the mine, and the mountain roads produced many fatal car crashes, including one that killed my uncle when he was just twenty-five.

Despite this, and besides some bullying, I had a fairly good childhood. I was taught to love God and country, and experienced the value of hard work.

During my childhood, people sat on the front porch and when others would walk past they actually chatted for a while. They shared vegetables from their gardens and helped each other during crises. My aunt Jeanne Mullins made footies for what seemed like every baby that was born within a twenty-mile radius. The minister even pulled a pair out of his pocket as he did the eulogy at her funeral. Nearly everyone in attendance raised their hands, acknowledging they had gotten a pair of those footies at one time or another.

Both of my parents taught me that serving is the highest form of gratitude. My mother was active in the community preparing food for showers, funerals, and those in need. Making sure that our neighbors were well taken care of.

My dad was a member of the volunteer fire department and serves as chief to this day. Growing up, Dad took care of two elderly widows by repairing their appliances, shoveling snow from their driveways, and doing anything else that needed to be done.

In 1977, a flood hit the area hard and ruined many homes. FEMA never arrived. But my dad, with members of the community and fire department, went house to house, pumping water from basements, cleaning, and spraying carpets and rugs. I helped my dad, and I remember getting home after midnight so tired that I could barely walk into the house. Nonetheless, I was so proud that night, knowing I was able to help people during a time of devastation.

I felt the powerful intrinsic reward of service without motivation for personal gain early in my life, and it put a seed inside of me.

> DL #2: If you are not serving, you are not leading. Make service a part of everything you do.

COAL TRUCKS

My dad had two coal trucks. One of the most exciting parts of my childhood was when he would let me ride along with him.

I had a vivid imagination, so I would pretend that the plastic top of a Folgers coffee can was a steering wheel and I was driving the truck myself.

Dad's entrepreneurship came with a price: He had to repair and service his own trucks. This was particularly difficult since he didn't have a garage. There were times when he would work deep into the night on a truck in the backyard, sleep a couple hours, and then do it all again.

Most of the time I spent with my dad was when I helped him work on the coal trucks. He often had to grease the axles of the trucks. The grease was in a large bucket with a pump handle on the top.

Dad would put the nozzle on a fixture under the truck and say, "Okay!"

With all the strength I could muster, I would push the lever down. It took five to ten seconds for me to force the grease out of the nozzle.

It was tough work, but I was proud that I was helping my dad. It wasn't until I was an adult that I learned he was just allowing me to help so he could spend time with me. He eventually told me how he could have greased the truck in half the time without me.

Okay, I get it, but I'm not sure why he had to ruin the memory of our great business partnership. You can bank on one thing, I'm never helping him grease another truck! Sorry, Dad.

DL #3: Be patient with the progress of new employees. Effective onboarding requires time and patience.

CASKET IN THE LIVING ROOM

There were some strange traditions in the coalfields. When someone died, his or her casket would often be taken back to the family home for the wake. People would shuffle in and out of the living room to view the corpse and just hang out, eat, and talk. I think some people enjoyed the gatherings.

There were always a few people who agreed to stay up all night with the corpse. They even snapped a few Polaroids of the body. It's a good thing we didn't have smart phones, or the Internet would be full of pictures of dead bodies!

I still remember standing in the living room of a dead guy in a casket. Of course, I was mesmerized. My parents didn't notice that all I could do was stare at the corpse.

At some point, a fly started crawling in and out of his nose. I wanted to kill that fly so badly, so I began to formulate a plan. I looked around, and, sure enough, hanging on a nail in the wall was a flyswatter. I stared at the flyswatter and then at the dead guy.

The flyswatter.

The dead guy.

I slipped over and took it off of the nail, hid it behind my back, and slowly approached the casket.

I kept waiting for the room of adults to clear and for the fly to land on the edge of the coffin – neither happened.

Somehow, I came to my senses and realized that, if I got caught, I would forever be known as the kid who hit a dead guy with a flyswatter. I gave up on the quest.

When you're a kid, you just accept abnormality as normalcy. As I got older, I started to question this odd tradition, and no one could give me a viable answer. I soon realized if you never question things, they may never change. Fortunately, at some point residents began using funeral homes for the wakes and funerals, and this strange tradition has faded away.

> DL #4: Don't be afraid to question company policies or programs that are outdated or seem to serve no purpose. If it has no value, change it.

I SHOULD'VE GONE SKINNY DIPPING

We spent a lot of time in the mountains playing Cowboys and Indians back when it wasn't politically incorrect. We looked for snakes and any other creatures we could find, fished, and most kids swam in the river.

But because some waste flowed into the river, my mother wouldn't allow me to swim.

One day while my parents were gone, I went down to the swimming hole with the other kids. Most of them were skinny dipping, but I was too embarrassed, so I'd grabbed a pair of blue jean shorts from home. I don't think I had actual swim trunks. I jumped in and had a great time swimming and diving off of rocks.

But then some girls came down to the river, and my buddies had to stay underwater.

So... I intentionally got out several times, dove off a rock, and dared my buddies to do the same. Much to my delight, they made some funny excuses to stay in the water. Finally, the girls left, and the naked diving resumed. It was a great day!

When I got home, I hid the wet shorts behind an old filing cabinet on the back porch, thinking I would get them later after they dried out. The perfect crime! Of course, I forgot about them.

A few weeks later, my mother decided to paint the porch and moved the filing cabinet. When she pulled out the shorts, they were as stiff as a board, and she knew why. Busted!

DL #5: Never withhold important information from your superiors. This will damage trust, minimize your influence, and might even get you fired.

VISIONS OF A THIRD GRADER

As far as ambition is concerned, I remember sitting in my third-grade class, staring out of the window and imagining that the trees were soldiers. I was at the brink of leading my men into battle when I realized that our teacher, Ms. Brenda Ward—yes, we're related—was asking a question.

She asked each student what they wanted to be when they grew up.

Most of the girls said they wanted to be a teacher or a nurse, and most of the boys said they wanted to be a basketball coach, drive a coal truck, or work in the coal mine.

The one thing I knew for sure was that I wanted nothing to do with coal. I had seen men coming out of the coal mine covered in coal soot from head to toe.

I still have much respect for those miners. Can you imagine crawling deep into a mountain eight hours a day for twenty, thirty, or forty years to provide for your family? Even after these men had taken a shower, it was next to impossible to clean away all the coal dust from around their eyes and the grease from under their fingernails. That was the life of a coal miner, and everyone just accepted it.

But even back in the third grade, I was different. My ideas were grandiose, and I wanted it all. I could see myself having my own company, traveling on my own jet, having a million dollars, or at least living in a big city. To avoid embarrassment, though, I scaled it back a bit and told the teacher I wanted to be a basketball coach or maybe a fireman. The bottom line is, I had a strong desire on the inside to do something major, hence I was on a quest to make my dreams come true.

DL #6: Effective leaders strive for greatness and do not allow small thinkers to obstruct their pursuit.

EVEL KNIEVEL

I started riding a mini-bike when I was five years old. This was exhilarating, since most of the older boys in the neighborhood had mini bikes or larger motorcycles, and I wanted to fit in.

Although some of the trails were scary, I took my chances. During this time, there was this guy who called himself Evel Knievel.

He wore what looked like a superhero costume and made crazy jumps on a super cool motorcycle. He jumped cars, buses, and at one point, attempted to jump the Snake River Canyon. He had broken nearly every bone in his body, but he never gave up. This was one of the most exciting and bewildering things I had ever seen. Of course, I began to idolize him.

One day some older boys and I built a ramp, so we could perform a short jump over a couple of boxes with our bikes. In an attempt to gain some respect, I volunteered to go first.

There was one small problem: I didn't know that a mini-bike wasn't designed to jump. But I would soon learn.

I stationed my bike about fifty feet from the ramp, wishing I had worn a cape. I could visualize my bike in the air with my cape flowing in the wind like Evel or Superman. As I looked on, however, I started getting nervous. My heart was pounding, and I thought to myself, how does Evel do it?

Just as I was about to back out of the whole idea, the guys started cheering me on. Go! Go! Go!

I couldn't chicken out now.

I took a deep breath and opened the throttle to the max. I zoomed the fifty feet to the ramp. As I came off the ramp, I didn't quite look like Evel Knievel soaring through the air. Instead, my front tire did a nose dive straight down as if gravity had a grudge against me.

At that point, the bike completely flipped and the exhaust pipe landed on the side of my calf. It was hot as fire and my skin started to scorch. I pushed the bike off as fast and hard as I could, but it was too late. I was blistered and screaming at the top of my lungs. Forget my reputation, I needed my mama! Some of the older boys carried me home and others pushed my bike. When my mother saw what had happened, she threatened never to let me ride my mini-bike again. That was quite a lesson. You can still see part of the scar to this day.

DL #7: Always examine the reasons behind your actions. If it's solely to impress someone, don't do it!

DROP THE COMB

I got my first real exposure to courage and leadership in elementary school. For whatever reason, when kids wanted to join a game of tag, they would approach me or a kid named Ricky for permission. I wasn't sure why, but I played the part enthusiastically. I was like the godfather of the playground. But even the godfather had rough days. In the fourth grade, I was exposed to the dirty side of leadership—or at least the opportunity to lead.

One day I strolled into the bathroom after lunch to find some older kids bullying a very shy kid named Roy. They had taken Roy's comb and were pushing him around, pushing him into stalls, and taunting him.

I instinctively demanded that they return the comb.

The alpha bully was a new kid named Juddy. Now, I don't know if his momma didn't love him enough or if it was the hundred-pound chip on his shoulder, but this kid was nasty. Juddy asked what I was going to do about it.

My heart was pounding! I started to get that adrenaline dump and tunnel vision right before you faint, but I said, "I'm going to take it back!"

Juddy scowled at me for a few seconds. No doubt he was scoping me out to see if I would actually follow through. He finally threw the comb on the bathroom floor, and he and his crew of Lost Boys stormed out in defeat.

Victory was ours! I was light-headed, and my knees were shaking for what felt like hours, but I was very proud of my act of valor. Of course, I remained nervous that Juddy and the Lost Boys would retaliate, but fortunately they didn't. Roy became a loyal friend for many years. And, as luck would have it, Juddy transferred to a different school. Problem solved.

DL #8: Stand up to bullies in your organization. There will always be those who don't play well with others, and they must be dealt with.

IN MANAGERS WE TRUST

As a kid, you generally believe that your dad is a superhero, and you trust adults...or, at least, most adults.

When it snowed, living in the mountains became especially fun, but challenging. One memory is quite vivid. When we needed groceries, we had to drive about thirty miles to the nearest town. Although we had one locally owned store, the supplies were limited. Since a snowstorm was on the horizon, my dad suggested we drive to the grocery store to get stocked up.

My mother was terrified of icy roads, but dad assured her we could make it to the store and get home before the roads were bad. As soon as we pulled out, it started snowing heavily. Mom wanted to turn around and go home, but dad reminded her that he had years of experience driving a coal truck in the snow. At first, we didn't have any problems on the curvy, mountainous road, but as we neared the top of the mountain the car tires started to spin. Dad began to touch the brakes lightly and then alternate by pressing the accelerator.

This didn't work. The car started to slide backwards.

It kept sliding until it was near the edge of the mountain. If it had slid any farther, we surely would have been goners. My mom was screaming and praying. Finally, just as the tires went off the asphalt onto the gravel at the edge of the mountain, the car stopped.

Then dad was able to get the car moving forward again, very slowly. We made the journey.

The whole ordeal was nerve-racking, but at the end of the day, I believed that Dad knew what he was doing and would get things under control. Thinking back, we probably had enough food to survive, so why would he put us at risk? Maybe I'll ask him.

DL #9: There are times when you must trust the process and the decision maker. Assume positive intent instead of malice.

DON'T WASTE BOREDOM

Growing up with limited commercial facilities or employment opportunities actually promoted creativity. Relationships were more intimate and meaningful, or at least it seemed so.

There weren't as many distractions. Those were the days when we actually looked into each other's eyes instead of down at our cell phones. Maybe I'm being nostalgic, but imagine having no video games—unless you count Atari—only three channels—I had to wait a full week to see if the caped crusaders would escape the Joker's giant wheel of death—and there was no mall, park, or other central place for kids to gather.

Naturally, we played a lot of sports, but we also participated in other fun activities. Sometimes we planned ahead but other times we came up with ideas on the fly. Either way, we always had something to do.

There were a million scenarios that could be played out at any time, and with any object. A towel around my neck transformed me into Batman—not Robin—insects could be monsters, sticks could be logs, rocks could be boulders, and grass could be trees.

One of the coolest pastimes was a secret town that we built when we found about three feet of crawl space under the old store building near my house.

We gathered every Tonka truck, bulldozer, and car we could find. Over time, that space became a little town and a full-blown construction site. We always encouraged new ideas, and these ideas kept the little town fresh and ever-changing. The interesting part is that no one else knew our secret town existed. Thank God the old store didn't collapse, because our parents thought we were out and about—not three feet below them.

DL #10: Cultivate a workplace culture where new ideas are welcomed and heard. Sometimes our greatest brilliance is found when we step away from routine.

THE SUPPLY GUY

When I was about eleven, an older kid named Jeff Brown, who still remains one of my good friends, some other kids, and I built a tree house that was quite impressive. It had a secret lookout with a sliding window. We ran a power cord so we had lights and music, and we outfitted it with some chairs, a table, and makeshift cabinets. It became the coolest place to hang out in the whole community.

I purchased all of the supplies needed to build our tree house by using my dad's line of credit at the locally owned store. I charged everything. I'm sure the store owner thought my dad had sent me to pick up the supplies. It got fairly expensive—we later found out one of the kids who helped build the tree house was intellectually challenged and had hammered twenty to thirty nails into each board. Even though I was fairly popular with the kids for my ability to fund our project, when my dad got the bill he wasn't in my fan club. Let's just say a good whoopin' wasn't considered child abuse back then, and my backside was red for a couple of days. Even so, it was pretty cool for a while since the other guys saw me as the "supply guy."

> DL #11: Mishandling finances is one of the biggest mistakes a manager can make. Make sure you and your team understand the ethics and policies for the use of company resources.

OUTGUNNED

Despite an otherwise wholesome childhood, life wasn't all fun and games. In a darker memory, four kids started walking me to the bus every day while punching me in the arm. I had bruises on my shoulder for more than two months, and my arm looked like Rocky Balboa's face at the end of *Rocky I, II,* or *III,* etc.

One day my mother pressured me for an explanation. She realized the consistent bruising in the same spot wasn't a coincidence. I hesitated and began to weigh my options. I knew if my mother reported the boys to the principal, I would be an outcast at school and would probably receive even more severe beatings. At this point, however, I was desperate. With tears in my eyes, I told her the truth.

After I'd finally told her, she asked Jeff—who helped build the tree house, to walk me to the bus.

This was a great turn of events! As long as Jeff was with me, no one messed with me. Things were so good that I began to strut past the bullies with an "I'm the man" look on my face. Everything was fine, until one afternoon Jeff had a Boy Scout meeting after school and couldn't walk me to the bus.

Uh-oh.

I remember trying to be a ninja—bobbing, weaving, and ducking in and out of trees and shrubs. I almost made it, and then—

There they were.

Crap!

More bruises!

DL #12: Staff your weaknesses, as you don't want to be surrounded with those employees who are just like you. Diversity brings strength.

BETTER ODDS

After a few weeks of beatings at the bus, I'd had enough.

Two of the bullies were twins. They were shorter than me, so I wasn't afraid of them when they didn't have their posse around.

One day, they decided to bully me by themselves without their pack. They started pushing me around and asked what I was going to do about it. I got up the nerve and pushed one of them as hard as I could—not sure which one, as I couldn't tell them apart—and he fell to the ground. I was amazed that I'd had the strength to push him down. I felt much more confident.

When I approached the other one, he turned and ran away. It felt so good that I treated myself to a Milky Way candy bar when I got home. After that incident, all four of the boys stopped bullying me.

Although they left me alone, I hadn't escaped completely. There were some other bullies who would pay me a visit in the future.

DL #13: There are situations when corporate or headquarters may not provide the support you need. This does not relieve you from doing what is right, even if you're flying solo.

LAND MINES

My all-time favorite sport is basketball.

There were several outside basketball courts throughout the neighborhood. And I use the word "court" loosely—more like an electrical pole with a basketball hoop or bicycle rim attached. While I did a lot of fun things as a kid, I usually played basketball two to three hours a day. I always tried to join the game where the older boys were playing, as the competition was fierce.

Jackie and Harold were brothers. They were dirt poor and lived between me and my favorite place to play. They were skinny, had rotten teeth, and apparently didn't like me.

One day I was riding my bicycle up the road to shoot some hoops.

Ding. It sounded like a piece of gravel hit my bicycle. This was nothing strange, since gavel flew up and hit my bike regularly, so I kept peddling.

Ding.

This time, I looked around. There were Jackie and Harold, taking turns with a BB gun, shooting at me.

By the time I realized where they were, I was too close to turn around. I had to ride right past them.

I closed my eyes and peddled as hard and fast as I could. I have never peddled so hard in my life. I tightened up, held my breath, and waited for a BB to hit me. They shot again and missed. At this point, I peeked out of one eye and saw them as I rode past.

Thank God, they either missed again or ran out of BBs. I'd made it!

From that point forward, I took what we called the "back road" to go to my favorite basketball spot. It was an old gravel road, much more difficult to bike on than my previous path.

I hated those boys and wanted to beat the crap out of them.

Later in life, I realized they endured a terrible home life and barely had enough money for food. I, on the other hand, grew up in a middle-class family and had a bicycle and decent clothes. I probably looked rich to them, so they took action out of jealousy.

DL #14: Understand staff personalities and their journeys before you react too harshly. The more a manager understands his or her employees, the more effective he or she can be in coaching the individual.

CHAPTER 2: MIDDLE SCHOOL

JUNK AND GLASS

In junior high, I was becoming more popular. This was great! I had some charisma, was a good basketball player, and enjoyed my growing popularity. But I think that made me more of a target with the older kids. I soon realized this quasi-leadership role that I was playing wasn't always pleasant and required courage.

As I said, part of my popularity came from being a good athlete. Although I had talent, I was skinny, so I was bestowed with the nickname "runt."

At one point in the eighth grade, I was on a school bus returning from basketball camp. I had broken my foot and was wearing a cast. On this particular trip, both varsity and junior varsity boys were on the same bus. The older guys were always doing things to the younger guys, which they dubbed as "initiation." Since I seemed to be a favorite target, some of the varsity players grabbed me, pulled down my pants—underwear and all—and pressed me against the back window, facing outward, in plain view of the cars behind the bus. You haven't lived unless you've had your junk pressed against a bus window! The fact that I was a late bloomer and had just started puberty didn't help the situation.

Although the varsity coach, Danny Yates, was driving the bus, the junior varsity coach, Al Hamlet (who later became an FBI Agent), sitting in one of the front seats, must have seen the commotion and started making his way to the back. Some of the older boys were standing in the aisle to block the coach's view. I was so relieved when I heard the coach yell, "What is going on back there?" As he made his way back, they quickly pulled my pants up and told me to keep my mouth shut. I obeyed.

The incident was one of the most humiliating experiences of my life.

Another time on the school bus, the varsity players held me down on the seat and, wearing their heavy class rings, beat me on the head. I'm sure I suffered a concussion from that attack because my head hurt for days. After that incident, as with the others, I told no one. Although they continued to call it initiation, knowing what I know now, it was more like felonious assault.

DL #15: The tallest trees catch the most wind. Leadership can make you a target.

FLOAT LIKE A BUTTERFLY

As the bullying continued, I knew I had to do something. It was a warm spring Saturday when I found the holy grail at an outdoor flea market—two pairs of boxing gloves.

I knew that if I was going to take on the older crew and stop the initiations, I had to learn to protect myself. So, I persuaded my mother to give me money for the gloves.

I started boxing with my neighbor Kenny Lester nearly every day over the entire summer. Kenny was a year older than I was, and outweighed me by about thirty pounds. He had some good boxing skills and usually pounded my head in, but I kept improving.

One day, Kenny was pounding my head in as usual, and I was mad. So I signaled that I needed a break. As soon as Kenny dropped his hands, I hit him with a haymaker in the face as hard as I could. Then, like any great warrior, I ran.

I was way too fast for Kenny.

There was only one problem. When he ran out of steam, he went home with my boxing gloves.

Later that afternoon, I looked out of my upstairs window and there was Kenny holding the gloves and taunting me to come down and get them. Finally, I got up the nerve to take the beating to get my gloves back. Getting that one good punch in on Kenny felt so good in the moment, but my subsequent headache said otherwise.

But what the heck. To this day I still think it was worth it!

Anytime I could catch one of Muhammad Ali's matches on TV, I would observe with a keen eye and try to mimic his style and finesse. I walked through the living room throwing punches, bobbing, and weaving. But in all honesty, I was probably closer to having Ali's mouth than his boxing style.

No matter what I had going on that summer, I always took time to hone my boxing skills. I would stand in front of the mirror and pretend I was getting bullied. I would say some cool lines to the bullies, like, "You talking to me?" Or, "You have no idea who you messin' with!" Then I would start throwing punches with lightning speed. Don't want to brag, but there were times I would beat up as many as four imaginary opponents.

DL #16: Build on your strengths and minimize your personal weaknesses. Never stop investing in yourself.

RUMBLE IN THE CLASSROOM

By the latter part of the eighth grade, I had gained more confidence. One day, I had my books under the seat after walking into class for study hall. A long-haired wanna-be tough guy named David came in and kicked them onto the floor. I picked them up and put them back under the seat. This happened two more times, even though I asked him to stop.

When he kicked my books off the chair for the third time, he also kicked my fingers.

Although I was scared of him, I had a temper.

Like a wild animal attacking its prey, I dove on top of him while he was still sitting at his desk. The teacher, who was also the basketball coach, had already started walking toward us so he was able to break up the fight quickly.

Believe it or not, the coach wrote a note for us to come to the locker room the last period of the day to have a boxing match. Imagine that in today's world?! Finally, I got my moment!

David had never donned a pair of boxing gloves. Better yet—or worse, depending on who you're rooting for—the sophomore boys were in the locker room and got to watch the match.

I ended up pounding David's face in. When we returned to class, the other eighth grade boys waited with anticipation.

When we walked in, it was obvious that I was the victor. David's face was completely red, and I looked exactly the same as I did before I left the room, just minus a little sweat.

Even better, thanks to the sophomores, word spread throughout the school. I felt like Muhammad Ali that day. I finally got a much-needed reputation.

While that marked the end of the days that I was bullied, the emotional scars have remained.

DL #17: If you prepare to win, most times you will.

WHATEVER IT TAKES

To get around, my buddies and I mainly rode our bicycles on the main road of town. It was fairly safe, but we had to keep a keen eye out for coal trucks.

I also rode my motorcycle up and down the railroad tracks, which was illegal. When it was warm enough, I rode my motorcycle three miles to basketball practice, sometimes with as many as two passengers. Nothing was going to keep me from getting to practice.

In one instance, I was transporting two boys and lost control and crashed. I ended up with stiches, one boy had several bruises, but the other boy, Tim Dotson, was 6'8" and merely stood up when the motorcycle started to lay down.

When we had snow days, my teammates and I would break into the school and turn on the furnace and lights so we could play for several hours before the coach arrived.

Interestingly, our coach never asked us how we got inside.

Maybe he recognized our dedication to the sport and decided it didn't really matter.

Let's see, riding a motorcycle without a license and breaking and entering. Somehow this didn't come up in my FBI background investigation. Sorry FBI peeps – must have forgotten about this until now.

DL #18: Often there are hurdles to reaching your goals. If there is not a door, break through the wall and build one.

CHAPTER 3: SWEET SIXTEEN

THE PERKS OF SUCCESS

I had finally made it through puberty when I entered high school. Before that, I had seriously started to wonder if all those Milky Ways had stunted my growth!

Better yet, in high school I got a car and a girlfriend. The freedom of picking up my girl in my Chevrolet Monza Spyder with the windows down and the eight-track tape player blasting AC/DC, I was the man! This was the height of exhilaration

Of course, with the car and a girlfriend, we took advantage of the situation. Sorry, Mom! But I was also completely smitten. My girlfriend and I talked on the phone until the early hours of the morning, and then we saw each other at school. Even though I got no sleep, I was invigorated by the fruits of love.

I also really liked that I was considered cool by some of the other students. I had a nice car, the hottest girl in school...who *wasn't* kinfolk—or was she?—and was on the first string of a championship basketball team. I was popular and loved it!

Unfortunately, I became quite enamored with my popularity. So instead of expanding my education and leadership, I bought into the idea that it was uncool to carry books home.

During my sophomore year, pleasure and popularity became quite important. My focus narrowed to just basketball, my girlfriend, and playing guitar. I had the world at my fingertips.

But it wouldn't last for long.

DL #19: To maximize potential you must minimize your social life. While it's great to have fun, success requires hustle.

TRAGEDY STRIKES

Growing up, I had a cousin named Jimmy Jr., known by the family as Junior. He was blessed with an IQ that was off the charts, and he was an amazing artist and musician. Junior could play multiple instruments. Since I could play guitar, we did what any cool teenagers would do, we started a band. Junior was on piano, Hobart was on bass, and Butter was on the drums. I think we played only one gig—the high school senior play.

Junior also played in his dad's country band on the weekends. During those weekend gigs, he was introduced to alcohol and started drinking nearly every weekend. I began to hear a lot of wild stories involving alcohol. Apparently, girls became very friendly if they drank enough.

So, by the time I turned sixteen, it was time to try some of this divine liquid. One evening, Junior hid two of the small bottles of beer known as "pony Millers" in his cowboy boots and brought them upstairs to my bedroom. I tasted beer for the first time...and thought I was going to puke. It was terrible— even worse than my first McDonald's hamburger!

Not to be defeated, Junior told me he could get some vodka. There was this drink called a screwdriver which required only vodka and orange juice. He was sure I would like it. We made a plan, and I persuaded my parents to let me spend the following Friday night at Junior's house.

Of course, I felt guilty about the whole thing, but wasn't about to change my mind. I told Junior I was all in.

On Friday, he drove into West Virginia, where he could buy alcohol at age eighteen. Later that evening, just as predicted, we mixed the vodka with orange juice, and it was delicious. I could barely taste the booze but started to feel the buzz almost immediately. I felt invincible! As the night progressed, we met up with some friends who were hanging out behind the school building. I felt cool knowing that I was part of the crew, especially since everyone we met up with was drinking and smoking weed.

DL #20: When that little voice inside your head is telling you "This is a bad idea," it is usually right. Sometimes small decisions can have a large impact. Don't forget: Decisions Determine Destiny.

Finally, it was around midnight, and we were nearly out of vodka. We stopped at Rife's grocery store, just 200 yards from my house and only a half mile or so from Junior's. We decided to finish the last bit of vodka and head to his house for the night. I remember trying to talk to him, but he kept the loud music jamming. We listened to LeFreak's *Funky Town* over and over. The eight-track tape had just been released, and he had purchased it earlier that day.

As we sat in the parking lot, Junior's dad was heading home from an auto auction and pulled in next to us, so we got out to talk to him. We did our darndest to hide the fact that we were plastered, and actually thought we had pulled it off. My uncle drove away, all the while knowing we were hammered. He went to my house and informed my dad. Within a few minutes, both our dads pulled into the store parking lot and blocked us in.

My dad came up to the passenger side of our car and told me to get out.

The minute I did, I was so drunk I fell against the side of my dad's pickup truck.

Dad helped me into the truck, and we headed home. When I walked in, my mother was waiting. She was a devout Christian who didn't believe in drinking alcohol, so I was extremely embarrassed when I realized that she knew I was drunk.

I proceeded upstairs to my room. As soon as I lay down, the bed started spinning. I jumped up, ran for the bathroom, and started hurling like a violent tsunami.

Then my worst nightmare happened. I heard my dad coming up the steps and thought he was going to beat me while I was puking my guts out.

I got up from kneeling at the toilet, went back and sat on the bedside, and looked at my dad. I started to cry and apologize.

My dad hesitated. I thought, *here it comes.*

However, he just said, "I guess this is part of growing up, and I hope you have learned a lesson."

I slept for a couple of hours, and at some point woke up with a jackhammer pounding in my head. After a while, my dad came back up the steps. He sat on the bed next to me and told me that Junior and his dad had an argument after we left last night, and that Junior had sped off in his car. No one had heard from him since.

Then dad left to help look for Junior, so I went downstairs and crept past my mother, who was in the kitchen. I took a shower and finally got the nerve to go into the living room and take whatever punishment, or exorcism, mom had for me.

Instead, being the loving person that she is, she made oatmeal, and I was able to eat a few spoonfuls, though my head continued to pound and my stomach was still churning.

After about an hour, several vehicles pulled into the driveway. One was my dad's. The door opened, and dad and a few other people walked in.

I will never forget the look on my dad's face. Then he said, "Junior is dead." He had crashed his car after the incident the night before and was thrown out of the vehicle.

I don't have the words to explain the pain and hurt I felt that day. From the wake to the funeral, it was nearly unbearable. The pain of losing my cousin and best friend was devastating. That summer was the most painful summer of my life. I was shut up in my upstairs bedroom for weeks.

Finally, Ricky Chambers, one of my best friends, persuaded me to go fishing. I remember sitting on the riverbank on that beautiful spring day watching the sun glistening off the water. At that moment I felt a glimmer of hope. Ricky didn't have to say anything. He was just present. I rarely talk about that dark period of my life and debated whether to include it in this book. But tragedy is inevitable and requires leadership. Think back to many of the great leaders throughout history. In most instances, it took tragedy to showcase their leadership. Be ready.

DL #21: In tragic situations, leaders must show up. Exercise the "power of presence."

'VETTE 65

After the horrible tragedy, my uncle was severely depressed. He had lost his only son under terrible circumstances. Since my dad had bought a garage from a mining company and reassembled it near our house, I persuaded my uncle to begin painting cars with me. He was very gifted, and we already had some equipment. It was a great learning experience for me, but we never made much money since my uncle would always agree to paint rust bucket cars for his friends.

During this time, I had seen an old Corvette. It was love at first sight. I knew intrinsically that I was going to get an old Corvette, no matter what it took. I started talking to my dad about it, and he told me if I could come up with half the cash, we would go and find an old 'Vette. He should have known better.

Now I was on a mission.

Observing my uncle, I had gained some skills in auto body repair.

I started buying beat-up cars, fixing them in my spare time, selling them, and saving the cash.

Soon after, I started looking at auto dealerships to find an old 'Vette. There was no internet, so searching for one was not an easy task. Finally, one day I was driving through a nearby town and saw a yellow 1965 Corvette Stingray. Hallelujah! I gasped for breath and could hear an angelic choir singing in the background. I had found my car. The crazy thing is, when I asked the price, it was only half the amount in the envelope I had tucked away in my pocket.

My dad worked second shift, so that night I stayed up until he got home. He walked in after midnight quite dirty from working in the shop outside the coal mine. I showed him a picture of the car and the cash in the envelope.

I remember exactly what he said to my mom. "Doris, I think we're in trouble."

The following Saturday, we drove about an hour and a half to the dealership, and, with a little negotiation, I bought the 1965 Chevrolet Corvette. I was ecstatic! When I showed it to my friend, Alan Honaker, I jokingly said, "We will get the girls now."

Since Corvettes have only two seats, Alan laughed and replied, "Not sure where we're going to put them."

Nothing is perfect, however. Although the 'Vette looked like a masterpiece, it broke down a lot. So what? To this day, it was the coolest thing I've ever owned. I sold it after I got married, in favor of a conventional house loan. That car is the only worldly possession that still makes me sick to think I sold. I still have the Virginia license plate that says "Vette 65." One day, I plan to find it and buy it back again.

DL #22: Leaders should have personal goals outside of work and take affirmative steps to reach them.

CHAPTER 4: LEAVING COAL COUNTRY

NEW JOURNEY

After high school, I received a scholarship to play college basketball, and played for a year at a small school in Kentucky.

Once again, I found myself in the middle of nowhere. Nonetheless, it was still college.

I was ready for some excitement, which included college girls. Slow your imagination, as things didn't quite turn out as I planned. For example, two of the first girls I met were wearing matching T-shirts that said "Skoal Brothers." I found out later that they actually dipped Skoal tobacco.

It turned out there were only a few girls I was attracted to, and the competition for their attention was fierce. Also, playing college basketball for a small college is not that glamorous. When we had an away game, we rode in fifteen-passenger vans, and some of the games were as far as six to twelve hours away. Freshmen sat in the back; it was miserable. On some occasions after an away game, we would get back at 3:00 or 4:00 in the morning and were expected to be in class at 8:00 a.m.

I also had work study to help pay for my scholarship, which started out as mowing the lawns at various buildings. Between practice, games, work study, and being the only guy on the team that wasn't from Kentucky, once again, I had to muster fortitude and courage.

Besides moving away from home, one of the biggest adjustments was establishing myself as a leader.

It didn't matter what I had done in the past. It was all about the present.

The other players couldn't care less if I had been popular at my high school or that I was a good basketball player—so were they.

Underneath it all, they wanted a starting position, and they certainly weren't going to let a freshman from Virginia take one of their spots.

As a result, I got several extra elbows and intentional fouls from the Kentucky squad, and also got into a fight at practice. The coach didn't seem to appreciate my fighting spirit. Even when I scored several points during a scrimmage, they ignored it.

So, I had to reinvent myself, which took time and lots of discretion. In other words, basketball, in and of itself, wasn't enough.

I had to find other ways to be respected, and I decided to take the high road. I complimented the other players when they performed well, even if they didn't reciprocate. I also encouraged other freshman players who didn't get to play as much as I did. This all took time and patience.

Unfortunately, during this time I had to face another bully. Of course, the other students had no idea of my history with bullies, but they would soon learn that I didn't take any crap! There was a freshman we'll call Silas, who was about 5'2" and looked like he was twelve years old. He lived in my dorm, and I soon realized that he was being bullied. One day, after a grueling basketball practice, I walked into my room, undressed, and lay down to rest. Just as I was about to fall asleep, I heard a commotion outside my door.

When I opened the door to investigate, one of the bullies was chasing Silas with a bucket of water. I demanded that he put the bucket down, but instead he threw the water in my face and ran.

I went ballistic and chased him the full length of the dorm, tackled him, and started punching him like a mad man. Yes, I brawled in my underwear—don't judge me. A bunch of guys pulled me off him before it got too bad. After the incident, Silas became one of my best friends. We even recently reconnected through Facebook.

On the bright side, the brawl in the hallway garnered me some respect. I am certainly not advising you to tackle anyone in your underwear, but you will have opportunities to put your courage on display. There is no better way to establish yourself as a leader than through the exercise of courage.

> DL #23: There are times when leaders cannot rely on past victories. They must establish themselves as leaders in the present. This can be done only through decisive action.

SPECIAL CHAIR

The college I was attending had a small creek that ran between the dorms and the parking area.

I could park my car directly across from the dorm, but to access the car, I had to walk about twenty-five yards to a bridge, cross over, and then walk another twenty-five yards back. This was frustrating, especially if I was carrying luggage. So…everyone came up with a plan.

Since the creek was not very deep or wide, one student could put a wooden desk chair in the middle of the creek using a stick, then jump on the chair and leap to the other side.

We'd then throw our luggage all the way across the creek. Then the next guy would jump on the chair and leap over to the other side. We used the stick again to hook the chair and sling it back to its original position. It was the perfect plan.

One Friday, my friend Bob Altizer and I were headed home for the weekend, and we did the usual chair routine. But at the end when I attempted to sling the chair back across the creek, my foot slipped in the water and I dropped the stick.

Since it was just a wooden desk chair, and other guys did the same thing, we just left it. No big deal.

We returned to college on Sunday evening and were told that we had been suspended for damaging school property.

We were shocked! Everyone did it. We went to the resident advisor's dorm room and begged to get an appointment with the assistant dean.

On Monday, we were notified that the meeting had been scheduled. We went in, did a mea culpa, and got reinstated into school—with two conditions: 1) We had to pay for the chair, and 2) We had to clean the piles of garbage out of the creek that had washed in over the weekend, which always happened after a hard rainstorm.

Cleaning the trash from the creek that day was a daunting task.

Not only did we fill about twenty-two bags of trash, but all of our buddies heard what happened and drove past, blowing their car horns and laughing at us.

Just when things seemed bleak, Bob got an idea. He confirmed that since we'd paid for it, we now owned the infamous desk chair. So, Bob started a raffle to give the chair to the lucky winner.

That's right—and we cleared about sixty dollars on the chair!

I will never forget walking into the dorm room one evening and there was Bob sitting on the bed, smoking a cigar with a wad of cash in his hand.

On a side note, Bob promised three guys that if they bought five dollars worth of tickets, he would rig it so they would win. When two of them didn't win, I thought they were going to kill Bob. He finally returned some of their money, so our profit margin went down.

DL #24: Turn your mistakes and failures into opportunities for success. Never give up! It's not over until you decide it's over.

KUNG FU FIGHTING

After my freshman year, I was so sick of playing basketball at a small college that I decided to transfer to another college. Since I had always played sports to stay active, I signed up for a karate class. I did that for about a year and even won a local tournament as a yellow belt. Then, as with most things, I wanted to be the best, particularly since I'd gotten beaten up most of my life. So, I found one of the best instructors in the country, Sensei Rick Smith, and started training with him. At that point, my life drastically changed.

The level of training was beyond strenuous. It was straight from hell.

It didn't matter if I had broken toes, deep bruises, or other injuries, I was expected to be in class, training.

There was a time when I started to hate Sensei Rick, but later realized that he was the most disciplined person I'd ever met.

Besides all the pain and time invested, the training helped me develop tremendous self-discipline.

I continued to train diligently and started to win tournaments. During this time, Sensei Rick went to Japan to train. Upon his return, he brought a new aspect to kumite, which means "grappling hands" or sparring, or as we called it, fighting. It was a different approach, where I learned to skip and cover more distance when punching or avoiding a punch. These new movements caused excruciating pain since the bottom of our feet became raw and tender.

After working on this new style of fighting for a couple of months, we went to a tournament. Some of the guys from my college wanted to go. I was a little concerned, as I had not perfected this new fighting style, and my feet were still sore.

Nonetheless, I acquiesced.

That was a mistake.

The next mistake was agreeing to ride to the tournament with those knuckleheads.

My first fight was against a little sawed-off Howdy Doody-looking guy who beat me. I was so embarrassed.

During the ride back—which I dreaded—everyone was quiet at first, until we decided to stop at a bar close to our campus.

After some libation, one of the guys started in on me. "Hey, Ron, you really showed Howdy Doody a thing or two."

Another guy said, "Hey, Ron, I think Howdy Doody has a piece of your ass in his cowboy boots."

My blood started boiling, but I tried to play it cool.

I blurted out excuse after excuse, which only made things worse.

Then I got angry and told one of them that I was going to break his neck.

After it was all over, I felt embarrassed that my friends had gotten to me. And although I have since matured, I still don't watch reruns of Howdy Doody.

DL #25: Pride comes before a fall. All managers should be able to admit when they're wrong. Some amount of vulnerability will lead to camaraderie with staff and other managers and will garner respect.

YOU CUT OFF MY LEG

Throughout my martial arts career, I suffered numerous injuries.

At one point, I tore a meniscus in my knee and had to have surgery.

But instead of waiting for my knee to heal, I returned to karate class too early and ripped the meniscus a second time.

This time, my leg was completely locked, and I had to go in for emergency surgery.

I wasn't expecting surgery and had eaten breakfast that morning, so the doctors couldn't sedate me with local anesthesia. Instead, they administered an epidural, which basically paralyzed me from the waist down. While talking to a nurse as I lay on the gurney, I realized that the medicine had done the trick. I was completely paralyzed.

At some point, I turned to my right to inspect what appeared to be a leg sticking up from the gurney. All of a sudden, I realized it was my leg, and completely freaked out. For a second, I thought they had cut off my other leg.

In my panic, I pushed the table with the surgery tools into the wall and began flailing my arms like a madman. At that point, the nurses and other medical staff dove on top of me and administered Valium into my IV. I finally started to calm down.

After they got me sedated, I was told the nurse had lifted up my leg to apply a restricting band to minimize the bleeding.

DL #26: Effective managers don't jump to conclusions without sufficient information.

CHAPTER 5: AND SO IT BEGINS

I'M THE LAW

While I had done many odd jobs before and during college, after graduating I embarked on my first career.

Although I majored in education and planned to be a school teacher/basketball coach, through a series of unexpected events, I ended up becoming a deputy sheriff. This was a career in which I had the authority to enforce the law and take away a person's freedom, and it seemed that people either loved me or hated me.

One of my first arrests opened my eyes to the real world.

I got a call about two guys who had been drinking all night and were causing a disruption behind a convenience store. When I arrived, I realized that these two winners were on the other side of a rotten bridge behind the store. Like a genius, I walked a short distance on the bridge and realized that I might fall through into the river any second.

When the drunks saw me, one jumped off the other side of the bridge onto an embankment and made his escape through a subdivision and into the forest.

The other guy started walking toward me with anger and hatred in his eyes such as I'd never seen before.

I was thinking, "What am I missing here? I have a gun and a badge. Maybe this guy will have a change of heart and surrender or fall through into the river."

He didn't.

Instead, he threw a roundhouse punch at me.

Fortunately he was drunk, and I was skilled. I blocked the punch and threw the guy over my shoulder. He hit the bridge so hard that it knocked the wind out of him. I thought he might be seriously injured, but as soon as he caught his breath, he began calling me names that I will not repeat here.

Finally, some other officers arrived but we had to escort the individual across a rotten bridge. He continued to kick and call us names as we progressed. I was afraid that we would all end up falling through the bridge, but we finally made it.

Until you've experienced someone hating you because of what you represent, it's difficult to understand things like that really do happen. After this episode, I started wondering if I had chosen the right career. I remain proud of the fact that I only used the amount of force necessary to affect an arrest.

DL #27: Remember, there will be some employees who hate the agency, and you're the company's poster child. They hate what you represent. Don't allow them to cause you to shirk your responsibilities.

HE SHOT THE SHERIFF

On the day I was sworn in as a deputy sheriff, I was given a Smith and Wesson .357 handgun.

But there was one small problem: I had shot a handgun only twice in my life.

Reassuring, right?

I was one of the few country boys who didn't have firearms growing up. For whatever reason, my dad never hunted and didn't own any guns. We were probably the only family in the community who didn't have an arsenal in their house. Nearly all of my buddies hunted squirrels, deer, or God knows what else. But not me.

After a couple of months, I started attending the police academy. Thank God I hadn't had to shoot at anyone up to that point. Although I was exceptionally strong in the martial arts department, it took me a while to master firearms. And I use the word "master" loosely. Overall, I did well at the academy and was elected vice president of the class.

My partner, whom I'll call David, and I had driven together to the academy every day as there were no dorms. We were nine weeks into the ten week training program when the unthinkable happened.

This was a Monday, and David and I had gotten called out to respond to separate incidents over the weekend. As we drove to the academy, he asked me if I had unloaded my firearm. I remembered that I hadn't. So, as soon as we parked, I unloaded the gun, put the ammunition in the trunk of the police car, and we walked into the academy together.

That day, we participated in scenario training or practical exercises, and were confronted with realistic situations with role-players to make sure we were ready to be cops. Since the academy didn't have training weapons, we used our service revolvers.

At the beginning of the day, we would form two lines, facing another officer. We checked our revolvers to make sure they were unloaded, and then exchanged firearms with a partner to make sure that all weapons were clear.

For some bizarre reason on this particular day, this safety practice was skipped.

During the final scenario of the day, the role-player, who was a deputy sheriff and had graduated from the academy a few years earlier, had a blank pistol in a pocket in his hoodie.

His role was to escalate the situation and then reach for the blank gun. Of course, we were supposed to beat him to the draw and demand that he keep his hands in plain sight. Since everything was alphabetized, David and I went last.

I went through the scenario and didn't have any real problems. At the end of the exercise, the role-player asked me if the next cop was the last one for the day.

I answered yes, and he said, "I'm going to rough him up."

As I walked away, David was walking outside. I told him, "Be careful. He's gonna rough you up."

I walked past the other officers and headed down the hallway to a window to observe. It was an old crank-out window, so I could see and hear the events play out.

The role-player started by pushing David so hard he fell to the ground. David recovered and, after a series of verbal commands with no compliance, drew his gun.

The role-player had his back turned and reached into the hoodie, pulling out the blank pistol.

That was when I heard a blast.

At first, I thought the role-player's gun must have fired off a blank round. But when I got a better view, I could see a wet spot just below the role-player's belt and to the left.

David had shot him.

My mind was racing! I ran out of the room and down the hallway, yelling to the other officers that someone had been shot.

While one of the instructors who'd been observing the scenario was rendering aid to the injured deputy, I ran to David. He handed me the gun, and it was literally smoking. When I checked, it was fully loaded, with one empty casing.

Due to the physiological factors and adrenaline dump associated with a critical incident, when I recall this event in my mind, it plays out in slow motion. We'll discuss this feeling in more detail later.

At that point, things got chaotic. The state police were called, and an investigation ensued. David and I were questioned as though he had planned to shoot the role-player. At first, I was stunned and thought these troopers needed a lesson in decorum, but I later realized they were following protocol.

Finally, after what felt like hours of interrogation, I drove David to the hospital, where he was given a sedative. Then I drove him home and spent the night at his house. I was deeply concerned about his emotional state of mind and didn't want him to be alone, particularly that first night.

David was suspended from the academy pending further investigation. He returned months later and graduated, but never fully recovered from the psychological trauma. The role-player survived but had a permanent limp. Despite the longstanding safety practices, there continue to be unintentional discharges at police training events every year.

> DL #28: No shortcuts. Safety protocols exist for many reasons. A manager's number one priority is to ensure that staff are safe. Review and practice.

SOMEONE CALL HAZMAT

Being a deputy sheriff in a rural area meant having a broad array of responsibilities. For example, one day I received a call that someone had apparently committed suicide.

When I arrived, I was directed to where the incident had occurred. I slowly entered the residence and had an eerie feeling. As I walked into the bedroom, I observed blood splatter on a bed and on the wall next to it. I started thinking to myself that it would be nice to have a partner with me.

There was a body on the floor, with an apparent gunshot wound to the head, and blood and gore everywhere. I waited on the volunteer rescue squad to arrive and helped them load the body onto a gurney. I can still see that scene as though it were yesterday.

After it was all over, the room where the shooting had occurred looked like a scene from a horror movie. When I called the sheriff, he directed me and another deputy, Chris, who had also arrived, to clean up as best we could. Us? Where was HAZMAT? Oh, that's right. We didn't have HAZMAT.

So there we were, trying to clean up with mops and a few trash bags. The bottom line was, we did the best we could. We didn't receive any instructions as to what to do with bed sheets, rugs, etc., so I stuffed them into several trash bags and placed them in the trunk of my cruiser, then took them to a secluded area and burned them with some gas and a match. That was the life of a deputy sheriff in a rural area.

DL #29: Effective leaders are adaptable and willing to do any job that is required for the team to succeed.

RIGHT AND WRONG

An incident happened when I was a sheriff's deputy that was both frightening and ethically challenging.

There was an individual who had what we called at that time a nervous breakdown. He had driven his son's brand-new all-terrain vehicle into a barn and set the barn on fire.

Another deputy and I were called to the scene, but as soon as we arrived, his wife screamed and shouted, "There he is! He has a gun!"

It was almost dark, and I turned to see a shadowy figure, pointing what must've been a gun in our direction. We immediately drew our firearms and took cover behind our police cruiser. At that point, he turned and ran into the woods. We didn't pursue him, as it would have been extremely dangerous running through the woods when we could barely see our surroundings.

The following night, we got a call from the individual's wife, stating that he was asleep in a mobile home adjacent to their house. To respond properly we needed at least three officers, but no one was available. Therefore, I grabbed another deputy, Steve, along with Raymond, a jailer, and we jumped into a cruiser to head to the residence.

We devised a plan, deciding that Steve and I would enter the mobile home and Raymond would guard the outside perimeter. Raymond was in the National Guard and talked a little too much about firearms and explosives. Hence, if the situation turned lethal, we didn't want Raymond on the inside.

Steve and I entered the residence which was completely dark, and quietly made our way down the hallway toward the bedroom where the individual was supposed to be sleeping. The plan was that Steve would shine his Maglite into the guy's eyes, and I would jump on him and restrain him.

There was no real creative way to handle the situation— skill and force were the only remedy. As we got to the bedroom door, Steve gave me the signal, and I kicked it open and ran inside. As I sprinted into the bedroom I heard a loud commotion, and a gun discharged close to my ear.

There was an open window, which the individual had jumped through.

After the gunshot, my ears were ringing and my adrenaline was to the max. I was afraid the guy had shot Raymond after he jumped out of the window. I yelled to Raymond.

No answer.

I could also hear the man's wife screaming, so the scene became even more chaotic.

Steve and I ran down the hallway with guns drawn and headed outside of the mobile home. As I turned the corner, I saw Raymond holding his gun.

He yelled that the guy had escaped. When I inquired about the gunshot, Raymond said he had shot into the ground behind the assailant in an attempt to get him to stop.

Since Raymond's actions were against policy and the fact that the blood was rushing to my brain, I grabbed Raymond, pushed him against the mobile home, and had a few choice words for him. Actually, Steve had to pull me away from Raymond.

When everything settled down, Steve wanted to talk to me in private. He advised me not to report the gunshot as it would surely cause Raymond to lose his job. On the drive back to the sheriff's office, I struggled with this dilemma but ultimately never reported the gunshot. In those days, if one cop ratted on another cop, trust would be lost forever. Still, to this day that was one of the most frightening situations I've faced, and I have to deal with the fact that I never reported Raymond's conduct.

Fortunately, the individual was arrested without incident the following evening.

DL #30: Where ethics are concerned, an effective manager always does the right thing, regardless of the consequences.

WINNING FEELS GOOD

While working at the sheriff's department, I continued to compete in karate tournaments. The previous Howdy Doody incident and two knee surgeries didn't stop me. As a matter of fact, I trained even harder and began winning numerous tournaments.

My parents came and watched me compete one time. My mother was appalled, and my dad said, "You're the only guy I know who gets beat up a thousand times just to keep from getting beat up once."

The tournament that gave me the most pride took place in Tennessee. My sister Becky had started taking karate and decided to compete too. This was a Taekwondo tournament—a Korean style— and I trained in Shito Ryu—a Japanese style. While there were a few other Japanese-style competitors, I was the only black belt, and all of the other fighters represented Taekwondo. It was a little unnerving being seen as the enemy, but also exhilarating, since I had been out-numbered half my life.

I won the middle-weight division. But as fate would have it, the winners from the three divisions—light, middle, and heavy—had to fight for the grand championship. I'd have to fight the other two and win to get that big trophy.

I beat the lightweight champion and fought the heavyweight champion in the finale. He was 6'4" and had some good skills. It was a good match, and we were tied two rounds to two near the very end of the fight.

At the last second, I sprang across the floor and caught him with a solid reverse punch. Finally, the foot movement that my instructor had learned in Japan finally paid off. Take that, Howdy Doody! I was able to keep some distance from the larger opponent, and, with quick hand and foot movements, I scored the final point.

The trophy was huge, and all other Taekwondo students were angry. That may have been even more satisfying than getting the trophy.

A few kids asked for my autograph. That was a cool experience.

The only negative that day was that it appeared a huge female fighter was going to kill my sister. Fortunately, she survived. We still laugh about that tournament.

I continued to compete in and win numerous karate tournaments, which included one where I beat the police academy director's number one student. That was extra rewarding since the academy director had told me his guy was going to mop the floor with me.

Eventually, after years of training, bruises, and a few broken bones, I became an east coast silver medalist and qualified for the AAU U.S.A. Karate Team. That was a highlight I will never forget. It had all started from a college elective, and there I was on the podium with a silver medal being placed around my neck.

Unfortunately, I didn't get to go to the nationals because I was "broke" and didn't have any more vacation days at the sheriff's department. At that time, karate was not a sanctioned Olympic sport, therefore we didn't have access to any funding.

Martial arts taught me many lessons, the most important being, the harder you work and sacrifice, the more benefits you will reap.

I often see many wanna-be leaders who want that big position overnight.

There is a time when you must work your way up. That time is always the most difficult and seems to last forever.

Climbing the ranks requires sacrifice, but if you keep moving forward, your hard work will pay off.

DL #31: The harder we work for something, the more we appreciate it. Actually, the best lessons are often disguised as pain.

PROGRAMMED TO LOSE

After a couple of years as a deputy sheriff, I got a position as a state probation and parole officer. This position taught me even more lessons in human behavior and emphasized the need to understand how people get to the point of making terrible decisions. I began to realize that some of these people had very difficult childhoods which left them with psychological scars. Many of them didn't know any other way to conduct themselves. It was as though they were programmed to lose.

I had to deal with offenders who had done everything from simple crimes, to robbery, to sexually assaulting a child, to murder. Meeting one-on-one with them was somewhat unnerving in the beginning. But, as I emphasize a lot in this book, when you do something repeatedly, you become more courageous. I found myself wanting to punch the child molesters, but I had to maintain control. By providing coaching, tough love, and strategic support, I had some success in helping the people under my supervision to change their behavior.

As fate would have it, one of my childhood bullies ended up on parole. Can you imagine his face when he recognized me? He walked into the courthouse to my office and told me he had just been released from prison. All of a sudden, his mouth dropped open and his eyes widened. He asked, "Aren't you Ronnie Ward?" I said, "Yes. Aren't you Jackie...?" I'm sure he thought he was a goner.

However, I had matured and wanted to help Jackie. As I explored his past, I learned he had been physically and emotionally abused by a family member and had gotten raped in juvenile detention. The first issue we had to address was trust. He made it very clear he didn't trust anyone with a badge. With this in mind, I looked for ways to build some type of a bond between us.

The most significant opportunity would happen organically. I had started supervising him a few weeks before Christmas. I don't know if you believe God speaks to us, but on Christmas Eve, I had this overwhelming feeling that I needed to get Jackie some food. It was beginning to snow quite heavily, so I had to hurry. I found the only store that was open and bought some basics—bread, milk, sandwich meat, chips, sodas, etc.

I drove to his house and knocked. He opened the door, and the house was cold and empty. I handed him two bags of groceries, and he looked bewildered. He invited me in, and we proceeded to the kitchen.

When he started putting away the groceries, he told me he only had one can of beans in the entire house. I had chills at that moment. He was so grateful for the gift that our relationship improved greatly.

Soon after, Jackie saw a counselor to help heal from his past. He secured employment, reconciled with his estranged wife, and started attending church. His self-confidence improved and, as they say, he became a productive citizen.

> DL #32: The past doesn't have to determine the future. Many employees bring psychological scars into the workplace. It is vital that managers recognize these scars and help the employee to overcome them and build trust.

STRATEGY

As a state probation and parole officer in a rural area, I had to learn how to navigate the different personalities and to remain acutely aware of the culture. Since we did not have cell phones, it was very challenging when I traveled an hour to see someone, only to learn the person wasn't home. Although I wanted to arrive unannounced, there were times when I had to call and schedule an appointment to avoid wasting so much time.

One time, I had one of five brothers on parole. I'll call him Frank. Every time I would call, I couldn't tell which brother answered the phone. When I asked for Frank, I always got the same answer. "He's not home."

I needed a new strategy, as I had not seen Frank in nearly a month. Had he committed another crime, used drugs, or done something stupid? I would have to answer to the judge about why I was not supervising him appropriately.

After a couple of calls, I had figured out the problem. When one of Frank's brothers answered the phone, I would identify myself. Of course, Frank had instructed them to say that he wasn't home. So, using my best Appalachian dialect, I called the house and said, "Is Frank air?"

Sure enough, one of the brothers said, "Yeah, hold on." Frank came to the phone and said, "Yeah?" At that point, I said, "Hello, Frank, this is your parole officer. I'll be over to visit you in an hour, and I expect you to be there."

There was a long silence, and I'm sure that Frank wanted to kill one of his brothers for admitting that he was home. I still laugh every time I imagine Frank's face when he realized it was me on the other end of the phone. While I'm not promoting trickery, I am saying that many situations require creativity, strategic planning, and adaptation.

AND WHAT ELSE?

Another lesson I learned was, when people had a positive urine screen, I didn't tell them the results. Instead, I gave them an opportunity to tell me what drug they had used.

Early in my career, I had a urine screen that returned positive for marijuana, so I asked the person what he had used. He admitted to using marijuana.

Then I asked the magic words: "And what else?"

To my surprise, he said, "And some cocaine."

Since cocaine stays in the system for only a short period of time, it's difficult to detect. However, with this admission, I was able to secure the help this person needed.

No matter what a probation or parole officer does, there are times when people go back to court, their term of supervision gets revoked, and they're sent back to prison. But most officers will strive to help them at all costs.

The bottom line: I learned not to play my hand too early.

DL #33: When managers ask the right questions, in the right way, they are more likely to get the whole story.

EVIL FANTASIES

A person I had on supervision lived in the mountains and had been convicted of raping his daughter. After the most violent incident occurred, his daughter began cutting her entire body. The only way I can think of to describe the cuts on her body would be like stripes on a tiger.

When it was all said and done, this man served only a year in prison for this offense and was released. After he had been on supervision for only a few months, his attorney petitioned the court to allow him to move back into the home. The prosecutor and I vehemently disagreed, but the judge allowed him to return home. No comment! Soon after, the daughter committed suicide. We all knew that he had violated her again, but he was never charged with another crime. As they say, a corpse doesn't talk.

The state asked me to be a pallbearer, along with six local police officers who were familiar with the case. The deceased girl's father, his wife, his son, and his only brother attended the funeral. No one else.

The day she was buried was a cold, snowy day, and the grave site was like a scene from an eerie movie. I remember standing at the grave, fantasizing about blowing the guy's brains out. I was certainly learning that restraint and control are paramount.

> DL #34: Emotional control is the foundation of great leadership. There will be situations every day that will push your psychological buttons. Just because you're "right" doesn't make you "right."

WORKING FOR AN IDIOT

After a couple of years as a probation and parole officer, I transferred to another county that was a little more populated.

Shortly after transferring, I had an experience with a quintessential poor leader. This person went from being a probation officer to chief probation officer without any supervisory experience. And, boy, did it show. His head was as big as an oversized beach ball. It was rumored that he had some political connections that had helped him secure the job. To this day, he was the worst manager for whom I have ever worked.

He was sharply dressed, nice looking, and seemed to be of average or better intelligence. Yet, he had one glaring problem—he was a narcissist. He made decisions to make himself look important to upper management instead of out of concern for his employees.

For example, one of the probation officers fell very ill, but this supervisor showed no empathy. Instead, he began barking out orders to make sure that the work continued to get done. The other staff already knew the work had to be done, they simply wanted a leader who cared. Because this occurred early in his tenure, he lost nearly all credibility right out of the gate.

DL #35: Employees don't care how much you know until they know how much you care. When an employee is experiencing difficulties, a quality manager always considers his or her wellbeing.

To make sure we met the mileage quota for the month, this idiot forced me and two other staff to drive three separate vehicles to a training venue over an hour away. It was rumored that he wanted to prevent us from talking about him during the drive. He routinely embarrassed people and touted his own abilities as an officer. The problem was, we had worked with him as an officer, and he wasn't that good. This man taught me so many lessons that I should send him a thank you note.

DL #36: Poor leaders can teach some great lessons. Keep a private journal on what not to do.

ANOTHER QUEST

One day while I was still a state officer, another officer and I were checking records in the basement of an old courthouse when a person walked in and introduced himself as a United States probation officer (USPO). What? There are federal probation officers!?

I later spoke with him for a while and realized that I wanted to work for the feds.

Another quest!

Soon after, I applied for a position.

This is a fascinating job that few people understand. A federal probation and pretrial services officer serves in the judicial branch of government and reports to the Chief U.S. District Court Judge. The officer is the first to interview someone who is being charged with a federal crime. After the interview, the officer makes a recommendation to a federal magistrate judge as to whether or not the person should be released on bail or remain incarcerated to await trial. If released, the officer supervises the defendant to make sure he or she obeys the law and makes their court appearances.

Next, if someone is convicted of a federal crime, to assist the court in determining the appropriate sentence, the probation officer writes a thorough and somewhat complex presentence report, applying the federal sentencing guidelines. This means federal probation officers are privy to investigative materials in nearly all federal crimes. I have some very interesting stories, but if I told you...

Finally, when a person is either on probation or released from prison to begin supervised release, the probation officer supervises that person, which requires a unique skill set. Each district has various specialized officers, such as sex offender specialists, location monitoring specialists, and some officers are involved with the witness protection program (can't discuss that one). The supervising officer is charged with protecting the community, but at the same time uses cognitive-based strategies to promote behavior change, explores resources to connect the person under supervision with needed services, and works diligently to provide overall guidance and support.

There are numerous stories where US probation and pretrial services officers change people's lives for the better.

Back to my story. I worked extremely hard on my resume, researched the agency, and spoke with another federal probation officer I had gotten to know. I also prepped for the interview and found out that the chief probation officer was a marathon runner.

After weeks of waiting, I was called for an interview.

It was challenging.

It took place in the basement of an old federal building late one afternoon and lasted nearly two hours. During the interview, I referenced my AAU/U.S.A. karate team qualification, which opened the door for the chief to discuss his running in marathons. Ah! I had struck a chord. We talked about exercise, our similar diets, and the thrill of competition. After the interview, I was drained, but felt very good about my chances.

A few days later, I got a call from a USPO with whom I had struck up a friendship, who advised that he had heard that I was considered the number one contender. This was during the same time period that I was working for the idiot, so that news was a ray of sunshine.

DL #37: Research the company and the interview panel, if possible, and prepare accordingly.

THE CLEANEST TOILET

While I was waiting to hear from USPO, I was having severe sinus infections and it was recommended that I undergo nasal surgery to repair a deviated septum. I wanted to go into this federal job with vigor, so I expedited the surgery in case I got the job.

While in outpatient surgery, there was a complication. After my nose was packed, I began throwing up profusely, which caused blood to seep through the packing. I had to wait for a while, then was sent home to my own devices. The vomiting continued to the point that I had to return to the doctor. They said it was normal—which I doubt—and packed it again.

While lying on the couch in extreme pain, I visualized myself as a fed—rehearsing what I would say to the chief when he offered me the job. "I am honored to accept the position, sir" or, "This is my dream job, sir. You won't be disappointed." It certainly lessened the headaches that I was experiencing after surgery.

Finally, the call came while I was recovering. This is it! My big break!

However, the call was not at all what I expected.

The chief complimented me on my resume and interview performance but said they had decided to hire someone who was already thirty-six years old and could not be hired when she turned 37. 36 is the age limit for hiring federal law enforcement officers. WHAT!? I couldn't believe what I was hearing.

My acceptance speech turned into, "Thank you for the opportunity, sir. If there is another opening, I remain interested." Just kidding. I have no idea what I said. Needless to say, I was devastated. I laid back down on the couch, hurt, angry, and stunned. Not only had I not gotten the federal job, but I was stuck working for the idiot who was making me more miserable by the day.

What did I do? I know you want me to say I sucked it up, got off the couch, and went back to work with a tenacity like never before.

That's not exactly what happened.

What actually happened was that I lay on the couch and got more and more angry. I had worked so hard to get this far. I had prepared. I had read numerous books to make up for my slack attitude in high school and college. I had prepped for the interview, worked extra hard as a state probation and parole officer, and was even told that I had the job in the bag.

So I sulked. I, Ron Ward, became a victim.

The negativity in my brain spiraled out of control. I thought about the most arrogant people, or brown-nosers, who always seemed to get promoted. I cared about people, but those types cared only for themselves. The more I thought about it, the angrier I became. Due to both pain and anger, I didn't sleep at all that first night.

After a few days of continued anger, hurt, and frustration, I broke. At about five o'clock one morning, I wept. Yep, cried like a baby. I also prayed and asked God to forgive me for my pathetic attitude. I promised Him that even if I had to clean commodes, I would have the cleanest commodes around. And I meant it. I recovered and went back to work for the idiot.

About two weeks later, I was at work in the old county courthouse when my phone rang. To my utter shock, on the other end was the same chief USPO who had interviewed me. He said, "Ron, we've had a miracle. The other position opened up sooner than we thought it would. Do you still want to be a United States probation officer?"

In shock, I rambled off something that may or may not have been coherent. Still, I managed to convey that I would accept the offer. Even more astounding was the fact that the new position was in a federal building that was even closer to my home than the first job was. I didn't even have to move. I was elated! Did I mention a nice pay raise, too?

DL #38: When you allow yourself to develop a victim mind-set, you cease to progress. Master internal thoughts, or they will master you. Practice gratitude, focus on the positive side of life, and hold on.

THE BIG LEAGUES

Soon after becoming a fed, I quickly realized that the level of professionalism was on a much higher plane. I knew that I had to up my game if I was going to be successful. At that time, we didn't have an official academy, so I attended a two-week orientation program delivered by the Federal Judicial Center in Maryland. Part of the training involved the federal sentencing guidelines that had to be applied when writing presentence reports. They were very complex.

After that particular block of instruction, I remember asking myself, "Have I bitten off more than I can chew?"

Before I had even attended the orientation, several individuals had been arrested, so I completed my first bail report. To my surprise, it was given back to me with so much red ink that I thought my supervisor, Dave Stevens, another one of my great mentors, had cut himself shaving while he was reviewing it. The corrections were not so much about the facts as about the writing itself.

This was embarrassing.

To prevent it from happening again, I had to spring into action. I found a middle school English grammar book and went to work. Once again, I realized that goofing off in English class had not served me well. Listen up, kids! After some time and hard work, I became an adequate writer.

> DL #39: If you're a smart manager, don't look ignorant on paper. Work on those writing skills.

EXPOSURE

To be an effective leader, you must have followers.

To have followers, you must have influence.

To have influence, you must get exposure.

In other words, people don't support or trust someone they don't know.

There were a couple of ways I gained some national exposure, which had a profound impact on my future career. A couple of years after I became a U.S. probation officer, I was asked by our training coordinator, Danny Kuhn—who apparently saw something in me—to travel with him to Dallas, Texas, for a "Train the Trainer" program.

I was very excited about this opportunity but had never before flown in a plane. Since I lived two hours from the airport and the flight was scheduled for 0-dark-thirty, Danny graciously offered for me to spend the night with him and his family in Beckley, WV. It was a great night. I played the piano with his daughters, and we all sang songs and talked. However, a treacherous snowstorm blew in.

The next morning Danny's wife drove us through the snow and icy roads to the Raleigh County Memorial Airport. Upon arrival, we learned there were significant flight delays and there were only three passengers for our flight— Danny, myself, and a local dentist. We decided to make the two-hour trip to the Yeager Airport in Charleston, WV, to catch a flight there instead.

Danny's wife agreed to drive the three of us to Charleston, and we arrived just in time to board the plane. Of course, I was pretty sure the plane would crash leaving the runway, but nothing was going to stop me at this point. After a connecting flight, we made it to Dallas. We checked into the Adolphus Hotel which was the nicest hotel I'd ever been in. Danny was quite frugal, so I ate a five-dollar candy bar from the honor bar in his room. But I digress.

The next morning, we attended the seminar, and I was amazed at the passion and level of professionalism of the presenters. I also learned that Danny was an integral part of the training, which garnered my respect. He later got promoted, and I got his position as training coordinator. I got to know several trainers within our system and remain in contact with some of them to this day.

A few years later, I attended a week-long FBI-sponsored defensive tactics seminar in Dearborn, Michigan. Since I had qualified for the AAU/USA east coast karate team, the techniques taught at the event came easily for me. The other participants recognized my martial arts expertise, and I made some great connections there, as well.

One of the instructors I met, Jeff Naber, was later tasked with selecting instructors to do demonstrations at the San Antonio National Safety Conference for Federal Probation and Pretrial Officers Association. I was one of his first calls. At the event, I did an edged-weapon demonstration.

After that demonstration, the floodgates opened. I returned to my office the following week, and the chief probation officer began getting requests for me to provide instruction to USPOs all over the country.

I started traveling more and more. That was great, but my work as a USPO didn't go away, so I had to find a way to maintain a work/life balance by choosing my travel carefully. Nonetheless, I had gotten national exposure.

What makes *you* stand out?

If you can't think of anything, then try and find your niche. Sometimes, it may simply be hard work, along with some personality. Whatever it takes, get that healthy exposure.

DL #40: Effective leaders realize they must put themselves out there to showcase their talents and gain influence. It's time to let your talents shine!

CHAPTER 6: HIGHER CALLING

GIVING BACK

I served in youth ministry at my church for a significant period. This was an amazing experience and I had the opportunity to help many high schoolers. So many teens need someone to encourage them and provide guidance, and I did my best to be that person.

It was also a great learning experience and kept me relevant—and I also got to explore my creative side. I wrote, produced, and filmed video segments, and wrote and directed skits—all of which coincided with the sermons. We built huge backdrops and filmed on location, including at local restaurants and businesses that loved what we were doing.

The most amazing part of this experience was watching teens migrate toward their talents to be part of this dynamic youth ministry. To aid their migration, I tried to place them where they could use their talents.

I learned that we had an amazing artist, so we started a newsletter and put him in charge of the artistic parts. Other teens played instruments, so they played in the worship team band. Some teens were introverts, so they worked behind the scenes on the video production. Some teens exhibited leadership skills, so they were given leadership responsibilities.

To keep all of this functioning, while also working full time as a USPO, I recruited several adult and young adult leaders. In most cases, these leaders would express an interest in certain activities, and much like the youth, they would migrate to their area of interest. We all did our best to provide guidance, encouragement, and tough love when needed. To this day, I am still in touch with many of the youth from that wonderful period in my life. One individual, Steve Gallagher, who has been quite successful, wrote one of the promotions for this book.

DL #41: A good leader gives his or her team members the permission and space to identify and use their talents, then fosters the development and celebration of these talents.

TAKING RISKS

In 2001, I made a huge decision. After all the hard work to become a fed, I decided to leave my job as a USPO and become employed by my church.

This was a major risk and many people told me I was crazy. Regardless, I was able to use my writing and motivational skills to establish a food distribution center and a teen center, which were all operated by volunteers.

In the rural area where I lived, we learned that on school snow days, some children had little or nothing to eat at home. As a matter of fact, many of the parents were addicted to opioids or other substances and weren't responsible enough to feed their children. We needed a creative way to feed these children.

While I'm sure this violated school board standards, we persuaded a few school bus drivers to deliver boxes of food on their bus routes to some of the most desperate families the day before a snowstorm was predicted. No matter what else you read in this book, this was my most important mission.

One of the most amazing parts of this experience was the significant number of people who volunteered to help at the food distribution center. I learned a valuable leadership lesson: People respond to vision and leadership, and most people find great fulfillment in helping others.

DL #42: Helping others is the highest form of fulfillment. Successful managers should always promote volunteer work.

THE MASTERS

In 2001, after I felt I had made a difference in my community, I returned to my job as a USPO. I sought guidance from the chief USPO, Dr. Sam Samples. I admired his philosophy and his approach to leadership. Before becoming chief USPO, he served as the Southeast Regional Director of the Federal Bureau of Prisons. He had many accomplishments under his belt.

As we became better acquainted, I found out he had a guitar collection. Since I played guitar, I paid him a visit. It was quite the evening. I played more guitars that night than I'd ever played before. It also produced a bond between us that continues to this day.

I sought him out as a mentor. A good mentor is not going to beg to invest in your life and career. As a matter of fact, some people say they want a mentor when they actually want a blueprint to get promoted. I sought his guidance to grow in my life and my career.

In return, he saw my hunger and gladly invested in my success. As a side note, a couple of years after I moved away, I received a huge package at the post office from Sam. It was a twelve-string guitar. I was extremely grateful!

As I continued to seek Sam's counsel on many issues, he encouraged me to further my education and obtain a master's degree. But I had two daughters, was active in another youth ministry, and of course had a demanding job. After much thought, I decided that was an impossible goal.

There was only one problem—I couldn't get it off my mind.

After wrestling with this issue for a month or two, I applied to a university. When I was completing the online application, the program froze up and lost my data entry twice. I was an inch from giving up on the whole idea, but I told myself, "I'm not a quitter."

When I finally got added to the roster, there were immediate writing assignments to complete. Once again, I had to make adjustments, so I decreased my television time—including sports—and set a personal schedule. I worked from 10:00 p.m. to 11:30 p.m. most nights, and intermittently for several hours over the weekend.

I have to be honest here. At one point, it all became too much and I had a momentary breakdown. Yep. I cried like a baby again. Afterward, I got some rest and climbed back on the horse.

The key to not giving up is planning, consistency, and, of course, having a good mentor. It's amazing what we can accomplish with those ingredients.

After many long hours, it finally happened. In December 2004, I received my master's degree—the boy who didn't take schoolwork very seriously had attained an advanced degree.

DL #43: Reaching that next level requires sacrifice, organization, and discipline. Also, seek out a mentor. In due time, you'll become a mentor yourself.

GOING SOUTH

In 2004, I received a call from Sharon Henegan from Washington, DC, who told me she was working on a plan to start a national training academy for U.S. probation and pretrial services officers throughout the country. Later, she went on to became the Academy's first director.

This idea was particularly exciting since the system needed a more robust training program. The current training was good, but didn't include firearms or safety training, driver training, or many other practical exercises that could be implemented at an academy. In late 2004, an agreement was established between my agency, the Administrative Office of the U.S. Courts, and the Federal Law Enforcement Training Center (FLETC). The dream of an academy came true.

In March 2005, I was selected to be a probation administrator/instructor at the academy, which had been established on the grounds of FLETC in Charleston, South Carolina. This was one of the most exciting times of my life. Goodbye snow scraper!

The original instructional staff was dynamic, and everyone realized the significance of starting a new academy. Imagine the pressure of starting something from scratch when many people believed it wouldn't work.

Each of the original staff added value to the training and brought a unique set of skills. Each one also brought confidence, and I quickly realized that this group would not allow the academy to fail. There is nothing better than serving on a dynamic team.

There were times when I led a team and other times when I was a team member. I learned something from each of the instructional staff, for which I remain eternally grateful.

On a side note, we had fun and there were many practical jokes, such as one instructor who broke into another instructor's locker and put talcum powder in his pants pockets. When he put his hands in his pockets, he was quite angry. It took a while to empty the powder. The fun continued when he started to leave and put on his hat. It, too, was filled with talcum powder, and it dumped all over his face.

The combination of the white powder, combined with the look on his face, were priceless. We eventually matured a little. Thank you, Sharon Henegan, Phil Messer, Jean Gabriel, Dan McClintock, Jeff Sanderson, Gene DiMaria, and Jed Blankenship. You all taught me a great deal.

DL #44: Never have too much pride to learn from your colleagues. A particular subject matter expert or thought leader may be in your company or already on your team.

NO SICK DAYS

Teaching at a federal law enforcement academy was thrilling. Yet, we had only a few instructors in the beginning, so the days were long. There were days when we would teach defensive tactics for eight hours straight.

I remember feeling like a zombie the first time we finished an advanced two-week instructor certification training program. I came home and my daughters were full of energy and waiting to go out for dinner. I told them to give me an hour. I literally lay down on the carpet for twenty minutes, got up, made coffee, and took the coffee to the shower with me. I finally mustered the strength to go out.

While I had many challenging weeks and months as an instructor, there is one program that stands out in my memory. The academy offered a two-week safety instructor certification course, and we had only three mat room instructors who could teach the program. One of the instructors, Jed Blankenship, was on extended leave, and the other instructor, Gene DiMaria, injured his knee shortly before the program and had to have surgery. We had to think quickly and managed to secure Carter Lee an adjunct instructor from Hawaii.

As fate would have it, the weekend before the class started, I came down with the flu - the kind where you visualize your own funeral. Since there was no way that one guest instructor could teach this intense program, I went to work anyway.

We started at 7:30 in the morning. I told the other instructor that I would teach my parts, then lie down during the fifteen-minute breaks. I asked him to tap me on the shoulder to wake me from my coma when the break was over.

I can't explain how bad I dreaded to get that tap, but I staggered to my feet and managed to teach my assigned blocks of instruction. At the end of the day, I could barely drive home, eat a bite, shower, go to bed, and get up the next morning to do it again.

Thank heavens, by Thursday, I started to recover and gain some strength. Over the years, I taught hundreds of classes. But that one will always stand out in my memory, and one for which I am most proud.

> DL #45: Sometimes leaders must dig deep inside to fulfill the mission. Dedication knows no bounds.

HOLE IN MY GAME

Many instructors at the academy would get together to do skill enhancement training, which included martial arts and boxing. Often, we would meet with instructors from the Coast Guard or Border Patrol for a workout. Since our instructors trained regularly, we could hold our own with nearly all instructors from other agencies.

One time there were some new federal law enforcement instructors from other agencies who wanted to spar, so we gladly put on our gear and joined the fun. Before we started, this loudmouth who was paired up with me started giving me pointers before we even began. I didn't say anything, but when we started sparring, I landed some really good shots in the area right above his shoulders—yes, his head. After a few minutes into the match, he stopped and basically wanted to know where I had trained. This was funny and fed my ego.

> DL #46: The old adage "Don't judge a book by its cover" can certainly ring true. Never underestimate your competitor's ability to outperform you. Keep your skills sharp.

One day, one of our instructors came to me and said that there was a guy from another agency who was a phenomenal martial artist. Behind my back, they arranged for us to spar. Thanks fellas.

When we began, I was faster than this guy, and I thought to myself, "Is this guy the best that agency has to offer?"

About that time, he took me to the ground. Little did I know he was a Jujitsu specialist. He worked me over on the ground like I was a baby getting my diaper changed. I was stunned! Nonetheless, I swallowed my pride and asked if he would train me and several of our instructors in Jujitsu. We began what is known as "rolling" or "grappling," which is similar to wrestling but with more finesse.

Before long we began to improve and developed a solid ground defense program. As a matter of fact, several other agencies came to observe our defensive tactics program, which incorporated boxing, martial arts, and Jujitsu. To this day, I would put our instructors against any other federal agency. Yes, I'm probably biased.

> DL #47: Effective managers will evolve and diversify their talents to move the needle forward in the agency.

THE NEXT LEVEL

After years of providing instruction on numerous topics, I was promoted to section chief, which was basically a mid-level management position. As a result, a new level of leadership was needed on my part.

I only had a few employees, and things went pretty well. We experienced many successes. I would later learn that this was not the norm. During this time, I certainly learned the importance of clear communication and encouragement. This was the ideal management situation, as I didn't have to micromanage staff. It enabled me to serve as a motivator, a team builder, and a planner.

Because of the successes I had experienced in this role, I began to think, "How hard can this management thing be?" Yeah, I see you smiling.

In my defense, the previous division chief/academy director always seemed to be on top of her game. She had this unique ability to make decisions, and she was a true visionary who possessed unsurpassed courage. Even when she had to make tough calls, she made it appear effortless.

She was a quintessential "boss." Of course, with the big office and her friendly smile, it looked like her life was perfect. Boy, was I wrong. I later learned that she'd had to deal with many dirty issues, just like any other leader.

> DL #48: Don't be naive. Things may be going smoothly, but that can—and will—change at a moment's notice. Seal up as many cracks as possible with the right policies, procedures, and culture.

WHEN OPPORTUNITY KNOCKS

I continued my leadership journey and remained ambitious, dreaming of bigger and better things to come. I read several leadership books and attempted to apply some of the principles I had learned. Soon I started to realize that some of the books were laced with fantasy...but we'll get to that later.

I worked very hard to develop what would be described in business terms as "good interpersonal skills." I developed curricula on various topics and always tried to broaden my overall knowledge.

I never limited myself to just firearms and safety. For instance, the academy needed a website, so I volunteered to build one even though I had never designed a website before. I had to make several phone calls to our DC technology office, but after some time, I put together a decent website. An employee with another office, Cindy Caltagirone, who later worked for me, cleaned it up the website to the point is was quite attractive.

After a few years, the top position became available: Division Chief/Academy Director.

The job duties of this position were broad and challenging. Not only did the position require oversight of all training at the academy, the division chief and his or her team provided oversight for the national firearms program, provided guidance on use of force issues, maintained data on all dangerous incidents involving U.S. probation and pretrial services officers, and maintained data on all search and seizures conducted by our officers throughout the country.

As for the interview, I had studied interviewing principles, I had my advanced degree, and I had worked to be the very best I could be, no matter the project.

Though I must admit, I was still intimidated.

Then, I remembered the advice of my mentor, Sam, who told me there are three reasons why people seek the top spot: 1) You don't want to work for an idiot, 2) You have the potential to influence the agency for the better, and 3) You make more money. As for the first point, I had worked for an idiot early in my career and didn't want to do that again. I really did want to make a difference in a positive way, and more money definitely wouldn't hurt. After careful deliberation, I decided to apply.

> DL #49: Don't you dare be unprepared for that big opportunity! While no one should do things just to get promoted, there is nothing wrong with getting better at your job and pursuing career advancement.

SELL YOURSELF

On the day of the interview, I remember waking up with a nervous stomach. The interviews were not conducted at the academy but at a federal courthouse about an hour from my house.

My mind was racing, but I managed to hold it together. I arrived, went through security, went to the probation office—which was awkward since I knew many of the staff—and waited to be called. I wanted to be alone to focus, but several people recognized me and stopped by to say hello.

Finally, someone came and escorted me to the interview room. I walked in, and a panel greeted me. Fortunately, I knew everyone on the panel, which certainly helped. I started with a humorous story about my daughter prepping me for the interview, which got a chuckle and calmed my nerves.

This was it—the biggest opportunity of my life.

It turned out that I was able to articulate my experience and showcase my sense of humor and knowledge of the job. It all came together, and I felt great. Although only a few days of waiting passed, it seemed like an eternity. Then I got the call.

I got the big promotion!

So, with a lot of hard work, dedication, preparation for the interview, and being in the right place at the right time—no one mentions providence in those leadership books—I got the big promotion!

Finally, the big office, a nice pay raise, travel, and a few other perks. It seemed surreal. The boy who probably should have ended up with a mediocre job in the coal mines had risen to this prestigious position.

Life would surely get easier after that. No more bruises or sore muscles, and if the flu happened to strike, this guy could actually take sick leave.

Or could he?

DL #50: An interview is not the time to practice humility. In fact, it may be one of the few times to boast about your years of hard work and accomplishments.

THE LONE RANGER

Now that I had the position, I was ready to take the world by storm and lead my team. No matter what the issues were, I was determined to pull the team together and stand tall. I would take the agency to new heights. I would be creative, motivational, and excellent.

That should work, since I'd read numerous books about promoting staff buy-in, how to embrace change, how to be a transformational leader, and the list goes on and on. I had years of varied experience, and I had been an excellent instructor. I was sure that if I exhibited integrity, met with my employees regularly, and conveyed a clear vision, they would love me and my leadership.

Guess again.

As you can see in the above paragraph, there were a lot of "I's" and not many "we's." I had a lot to learn about leadership in this new role. I was the team leader, but I needed to come to the realization that building a team doesn't just happen along with the title. It was going to take more.

Much more than I realized.

DL #51: Avoid using "I" where possible. Any business, organization, or company is comprised of a team. You may be the quarterback, but everyone plays an important role.

TSUNAMI

I began the first morning by reorganizing the big office to suit my taste. I did that for about an hour, and then started getting inquiries about budget projections, travel requests from employees, scheduling issues, equipment needs from middle management, assignments from my superiors, mandatory training that had to be completed within two weeks, and the list goes on.

In addition to all of the academy responsibilities, as division chief, I was also charged with overseeing the national firearms and use of force programs. In addition, I faced a very serious personnel issue that required a great deal of attention. This particular employee hired a lawyer—lucky me—and I had very limited training on the ins and outs of personnel issues.

I quickly realized that, for me to survive and manage all of these responsibilities, I needed a deep dive into organizational skills. However, that didn't come naturally for me. I'm the guy who could walk into your office with a water bottle and never think to take it out with me. I have been known to leave my credit card with the bill in a restaurant. So, I went on a quest to get organized.

When I arrived in the morning, there were certain things that were paramount, such as approving leave, checking my personal calendar and the agency calendar, reading priority emails, reviewing text messages, etc.

Nothing changes until it becomes a habit.

So, to make sure I got all of this done, I made a checklist that helped make it into a habit. This sounds simple, but often when I arrived, someone would be waiting to talk to me. Next thing I knew, half of the morning was gone. The checklist served as a reminder for me, so at the next free moment I was on it.

Next, I started to journal with an old-school paper and pen. I noted important things to do, conversations, meetings, etc. This worked well at first, but when I referred to the journal a month or two later, I couldn't understand my own notes.

I realized the notes needed more specific information. To enhance my notations, I added the date, the issue or person, and some details. I also used adhesive note tags on matters that might need attention in the future.

Next, I started snapping pictures with my phone regarding things I needed to remember.

These tools and strategies helped me to function more efficiently.

Years later, Siri became one of my BFFs. I proposed marriage, but she said she wasn't the marrying kind. Ask her yourself. I set reminders all the time.

New habits take time.

Let me repeat that. New habits take time!

With some discipline, trial and error, and consistency, my system improved.

DL #52: If you're not organized, you're not in control.

DAY CARE CENTER

Although I had gotten more organized, the pressure was immense. I started averaging about four to five hours of sleep each night, with at least one night a week when I barely slept at all. It was overwhelming.

Of course, to operate at a high level, one needs to be rested and have a good workout routine, a good diet, coping mechanisms, and stress-reduction techniques—we'll discuss this in more detail later.

While the daily operations were a challenge, nothing compared to the time and effort it took to manage human behavior. Frankly, I underestimated the immaturity and malice of some employees. Yes, I said it! It is mind-boggling the way some people are paranoid, unhappy, gossipers, divisive, and just plain weird.

I saw everything from a staff member who rose shirking responsibility to an art form, staff who just couldn't get along with one another, and an individual with breath so bad no one could work within three feet of him. Then you get the people with no filters and bad timing, hearing about how Chad hates his in-laws so much that he's considering moving away, or that Beverly's online dating experiences stink, or that Ralph has a boil on his backside. You get the picture.

While these behaviors are challenging to manage, I found that the negative personality was the most difficult for me, almost like mental body odor.

Once I was meeting with an employee who wanted to attend a training program but had already traveled five times over the past three months, so I denied it. He got upset and made some comments I didn't appreciate, and so I blurted out, "You should be grateful that you get to travel at all!"

While my statement was true, it wasn't the right statement for this occasion—it set him off. He said, "Are you saying that I'm not grateful?"

I retracted the statement but didn't give in and allow the unnecessary travel. If I had given in to those outbursts, I would have been ruined as a manager. In instances when managers give in to extreme behaviors, I call it managing personalities rather than managing employees.

In terms of human behavior, a psychiatrist once told me that you can change fifteen percent of someone's behavior through coaching, and the other eighty-five percent may require boundaries, policies, and directives. I believe he was spot on.

DL #53: Never forget: Some employees are toddlers in adult bodies. Not only will managers supervise all types of people, they will be confronted with bizarre behavior and will have to decide when it becomes detrimental to the organization and take appropriate action.

FIRST CONTACT

I was expecting some time to adapt to this new position, but quickly realized staff had immediate needs. They had questions, requests, and needed guidance on various issues. I did my best, but it was impossible to learn everything at once, so I had to take one issue at a time, provide answers, and help develop solutions. As I've said, it was daunting, but some of my early strategies proved to be successful.

How did I do this right out of the gate? I'm glad you asked.

Remember this: Do not fear.

If you don't know the answer, someone else will. One of the keys to my success was to establish a point-of-contact list which consisted of people who could help me to be successful. I didn't do this by phone. Instead, I got out of my chair and took the time to meet them in person whenever possible.

I had no clue how valuable these relationships would become. Every time I went to the main office in DC, I introduced myself to pertinent people, which helped me address issues and obtain support from a distance.

One of the best examples of developing contacts occurred when I worked for a judge as a USPO. The judge always wanted to know whether a person under supervision was making child support payments and, if so, when and how much was the last payment.

Normally, an officer had to travel to the county courthouse to get this information. However, I took the time to meet the employee who had this information and asked if she would be willing to be my point of contact for child support issues. She agreed. After that, all I had to do was pick up the phone and call her, and I could get the answers I needed in minutes.

Eventually, other officers realized I'd made a great connection and started asking if I could call my contact to get the child support payment information on their behalf. Unfortunately, they didn't want to take the time to establish their own relationships. I learned that by establishing points of contact, seeking guidance, and establishing priorities, the management onboarding process could be expedited.

DL #54: As a new leader, there is no grace period. Start establishing contacts, set your priorities, and don't get overwhelmed. You've got this!

THE BIG LEAGUES

In addition to everything else on my plate, I was notified a few weeks after the big promotion that I would have to make several speeches and presentations. Picture this: My first presentation was scheduled to occur in Brooklyn, New York, shortly after I was promoted in 2009. I had to address all chief and deputy chief U.S. probation and pretrial services officers—about 160 in total—in the eastern part of the United States.

My superiors advised, "Just share your vision for the future of training." No problem!

Then I thought, "Oh crap, what is my vision?"

I met with the section chiefs, and we devised a strategic training plan and put together a presentation. I practiced it a few times, and it seemed as though it would be impactful.

Then, out of the blue, a know-it-all employee from DC called me and asked if I was ready. I told her I felt pretty good about it. However, she strongly suggested that I call my superiors in DC and rehearse. She ended the call by saying, "You're in the big leagues now."

It can be surprising to new managers at first to get this type of feedback, but I recognized by her tone that she was just being condescending. And she wasn't even in a position of authority. She left the agency a few years ago. I sure hope she's not a motivational speaker.

A CRAZY RIDE

I arranged my flight to arrive in Brooklyn the day before the big presentation. But at the airport in Charleston, I learned that my flight had been cancelled. The gate attendant said the next flight was at 5:30 the next morning. With a connecting flight, I would arrive at LaGuardia airport at noon. I was scheduled to speak at 1:15 p.m.

So, I headed home, barely slept, got up at 4:00 a.m., and headed back to the airport. As predicted, the plane landed in New York at noon. By the time I went to baggage claim and exited, it was 12:20 p.m.

I couldn't hail a taxi, so I secured a black car cab. At around 12:35 p.m., I told the driver that I had to be at the hotel in thirty minutes. I think I made his day. He smiled and said, "No problem." It was a crazy ride, to say the least.

I checked in to the hotel at 1:05 p.m., ran upstairs, put my suitcase in my room, and walked down to the conference room just in time to get the lavalier mic attached. At 1:15, I was presenting. I was a little nervous at first, but I'm glad to report that the presentation went very well. In fact, I was the only speaker that day who received applause. I think one of my longtime friends started the applause, but I'll take what I can get.

DL #55: Effective leaders develop the skills necessary to thrive under pressure. For public speaking, practice, practice, practice. Use a mirror or speak to a small group of friends and family. Maybe your dog will listen!

NEW HEIGHTS

In 2012, I was elected chair of a federal law enforcement training accreditation board, which has the authority to oversee the standards of accreditation to ensure that all federal law enforcement agencies and select military law enforcement programs run in an organized and professional manner.

It comprises nearly all major federal law enforcement agencies throughout the country, including the FBI, Secret Service, U.S.

Marshals, DEA, etc. There is also a military presence, someone from the academic world, and a public member.

To serve in this capacity was a tremendous honor. I was among some of the most effective leaders in the federal government, the military, academia, and the private sector. At this point in my career, I had gained a great deal of confidence in my abilities—through self-development techniques which will be discussed later—so I brought my own style and personality to the position. I used my sense of humor and my ability to connect with others to advance the board's mission.

DL #56: It's not where you come from but where you're heading that matters. Many times, we allow our background and surroundings to make us insecure. Never be intimidated by anyone. They're just mortals.

In addition to the board members, the accreditation community is composed of volunteers from the various federal agencies that conduct assessments of programs and academies. These people are essential to the accreditation process.

As board chair, I always tried to convey the board's appreciation for the hard work of these volunteers. During board meetings, the community had parallel meetings and usually participated in a training program. The executive director and I always made time to leave the board meeting for a few minutes, walk over to where the community was meeting, and brief them on pertinent updates and answer their questions.

Many employees who represented the community sent me messages of appreciation, and complimented me for my approachability and style of leadership. During the board meetings, we hosted an evening social where the board and community all got together. Before meetings, I encouraged the board members to spend time with the community of assessors and express appreciation for their hard work. Of course, they were more than willing to oblige.

DL #57: Treat the janitor and the CEO the same. All human beings deserve dignity and respect.

As with any leadership position, there were challenges. For example, when an agency didn't meet the criteria for accreditation, as the board chair, I had to deliver the bad news and answer the agency's questions. Imagine an agency working hard and passing an initial assessment, only to appear before the board and be rejected. I must admit that notifying a major federal law enforcement agency that its initiative had failed took some cojones.

I was still serving as chair when the federal government enacted budget sequestration—creating significant budget cuts across federal agencies.

Things got quite complicated, to say the least.

I had to analyze two budgets—one in the judicial branch of government, where I served as academy director, and the other in the executive branch, where I served as board chair. This came with several difficult decisions, such as cutting training programs at the academy and reducing board meetings from three times a year to twice per year.

I also decided to cancel the accreditation board's ten-year anniversary celebration because Hurricane Sandy was approaching the Baltimore area. This was difficult because ten years is an important benchmark, and a lot of time and effort had gone into preparing for that event. We had secured a letter from the president of the United States to be read at the gathering, and members of congress and other dignitaries were set to attend the meeting.

I will never forget getting a call from the executive director of the office of accreditation, asking me whether to move forward with preparations or cancel the event. I had until the end of the day as numerous flights and hotels would have to be cancelled. I mulled over this decision intensively. I called my friend, the Coastguard Captain and asked, "don't you guys have some inside track on weather predictions?" He laughed and said, "you're on your own my friend." He was right.

I waited until 4:30 that afternoon and made the call to cancel the event. It turned out that the hurricane did a lot of damage. So, although it was a difficult decision, it had been the right call.

DL #58: Some decisions may be outside of your expertise, but a decision must be made. Sometimes you just have to trust your gut.

CHAPTER 7: TURNING POINT

COURAGE THROUGH PRACTICE

I had to face a lot after being promoted to academy director, but more importantly, I needed to adjust the way I performed as a leader. I needed a turning point. As I share mine, I hope it will serve as a catalyst for you.

Of all my responsibilities, the one that was most daunting was how to successfully handle employee confrontations. That was why I was so nervous when I had to terminate the employee in the preface of this book.

But, let me tell you, this might be the most important lesson of all in terms of courage. If confrontation is an issue for you, please pay attention.

This epiphany changed the way I managed people forever and was instrumental in helping me make great strides as a leader.

We teach many basic skills in federal law enforcement training. They are taught in the classroom and reinforced through practical exercises and scenarios with guidance from an experienced instructor. The goal is for students to succeed with minimal training scars, yet to make the training as realistic as possible.

As the academy director, I regularly tried to observe the classes and exercises, and I learned an important lesson that changed my life. I was observing a simulated lethal force scenario which required trainees to respond to a mock life and death encounter.

There was a new officer in this class whom we'll call Jasmine. I'd spoken with her when she first arrived for training and she was very, very nervous. She had never shot a firearm before. She had never practiced any type of self-defense. And now she had to perform in this lethal force scenario.

It was very realistic. The trainees approach a realistic-looking house responding to a domestic disturbance, and someone comes out with a shotgun firing blanks.

It's loud. They're blanks, but you can smell the gunpowder. It's scary.

Jasmine had come in nervous, had practiced and diligently followed the training, and now she and her partner were being thrust into the scenario.

Here is a new young aspiring officer who has never shot a gun before, never practiced self-defense before, and now she's successfully completing a scenario where an assailant is firing a shotgun at her.

How did she do? She aced it.

The diverse training delivery, as well as Jasmine's hard work and practice during the program had certainly paid off.

Then I had an epiphany. The same concepts could be used for less exotic daily functions of managers to help them properly deal with the anxiety that comes with making difficult decisions and confronting behaviors. It's not getting shot at, but sometimes needing to confront someone at work has made me more nervous than actual law enforcement situations.

You can learn to operate from a position of courage. And with practice, it can become second nature.

Imagine that. You can learn courage through practice.

Figuring out these principles led me to the next great chapter of my life. These were the principles I used at the academy, which in turn led to me write this book and form 4Ward Management Coaching upon my retirement. More importantly, I want to help you master these skills in the remaining pages of this book.

DL #59: Fear is the enemy and can only be defeated through strategies and practice. Keep chipping away at that wall.

PART II

SKILLS THAT MAKE A BIG DIFFERENCE

Courage is learnable.

And leadership skills can be enhanced.

While some parts of leadership are very personal, there are also technical fundamentals that you have to master.

Here I want to get a little more instructional in nature. I've even got some tables and charts for you. If you like that sort of thing.

It's technical, but it's not so hard. You learn it, you practice it, you get better at leading. I will continue to include personal situations to keep it interesting.

I want to start with five big lessons which examine what things will look like when they're running great and some of the fundamentals to get there quickly.

Okay, let's get started.

CHAPTER 8: A WELL-OILED MACHINE

Let's begin by looking at the top of the mountain.

A lot of managers are stressed, busy, frantic. Feeling like that story about the Dutch boy who must stop the dam from breaking by plugging the holes with his fingers. Their trying to go it alone and the team members aren't on the same page.

When you've got a well-oiled machine, everything gets done without you running yourself into the ground. Politics and disagreements are minimal, everyone knows their job, everything gets done, and you aren't going crazy in the process.

You want that, right? Well, why wouldn't you have it? Let's explore.

LESSON I

THE MONKEY

Early in my management career, the other members of the team and I were involved in developing complex schedules, venue availability, equipment needs, etc., for student training. This was a daunting task, and frankly, I wasn't that good at it.

I would attend meeting after meeting with the other managers to go over all the details. And there were a whole lot of details.

I wanted to show the team that, as manager, I was getting my hands dirty just like everyone else. But by participating in these logistical meetings, I had to work overtime to finish my other tasks.

One day it hit me: The rest of the team was perfectly capable of developing these schedules. My presence wasn't necessary.

Huh.

At that point, I wised up. I advised staff if they needed input or had questions, I would be available, but I would not attend the meetings.

This worked wonders for my schedule. Everything still got done right. Everyone was happy. And I wasn't going crazy working overtime on eighty different things.

Actually, I wanted to kick myself for not delegating sooner.

It seems like everyone knows that delegation is important, but managers often struggle with it, don't they? Come on, be honest, maybe you struggle with it sometimes.

Why do we continue to complete tasks ourselves when they could easily be delegated? There are a lot of reasons, but here's a sneaky one—the monkey.

The monkey is taking on the responsibility for a particular task.

If you're not careful, you'll place the monkey on your back when it comes to…well, everything. And yes, some staff will do their best to give you some of their monkeys!

Here's a good example. Headquarters needed an article on a particular topic to go in the national weekly update, so I delegated the article to the staff member who was the expert in that area. A couple of days later, he sent me a list of bullet points for the update.

But hold on. Who had the monkey now?

I did.

Since I had gotten better at the art of delegation, I sent it back and said, "This is a good start. Now put it into narrative form."

Don't allow the monkey to be placed on your back by others.

Delegation requires trusting your team, having the courage to lead and possessing specific skills.

TOM SAWYER

In simple terms, delegation is the process of giving someone else a responsibility instead of doing it yourself. Mastering delegation can be a life-changer, and it's key to getting a lot done as a leader and manager.

Remember how I said your upbringing and journey affects who you are? Take those lessons and ponder on them as we progress.

Here is one of mine—the first time I saw delegation in action. It was back when I painted cars in high school with my uncle and ultimately bought the '65 Corvette.

Well, one day my uncle had to leave the garage. He instructed me that while he was gone, there were two cars that needed to be sanded with sandpaper. That was the most physically demanding part of prepping the auto body.

So... I devised a plan. I told three boys that I was giving free auto bodywork lessons. They were excited for the free master class. I said we'd start with sanding the cars, and after a little instruction, they went to work. I got some iced tea and moved my chair close to them so I could give my brilliant feedback.

Everything was going well until my uncle returned early. He was stunned and did not appear impressed with my apprenticeship program. He inquired as to what was happening. I think the fact that I had my feet propped up on a milk carton and was sipping iced tea probably didn't help the situation.

I explained that I was giving auto body lessons to these fortunate young men. I think he admired my ability to delegate, but he was mad. He ended my training program on the spot and began calling me Tom Sawyer after that. But I did see my first glimpse of the process of delegation, even if it came almost accidentally, and ended up being a funny story all these decades later.

I see many people struggle with delegation for various reasons. Let's look at some examples of poor delegation to help make the point.

I CAN DO IT MYSELF

That is an old school idea that still gets a lot of managers into trouble.

Some years ago, a senior manager and I had to send a document to a colleague via fax. If you've never heard of a fax machine, Google it. Anyway, the manager got up and said, "Follow me."

We walked down a long hallway to the fax machine, document in hand. Then he tried to fax the document.

But, nope.

Again, nope.

He kept having trouble. I just stood there and watched him try time and time again to no avail.

At some point, I said quite loudly, "Do you not have anyone who can operate this machine?" A staff assistant heard me and walked up. Thirty seconds later, the document was faxed.

As we took the long walk back to the manager's office, I asked why he didn't get the staff assistant to fax the document in the first place.

He said, "I like to show the staff we can operate without them."

Many leaders fail to delegate because they think they need to send a message to staff that they can do any part of the job.

That is a dangerous philosophy. It undermines the very concepts of teamwork, coaching, and relying on contributions from everyone.

The beauty of "team" is the unique gifts and talents that each staff member brings to the table.

If you catch yourself saying, "I can do it myself," that's a great prompt to practice some delegation and get that monkey off your back.

EXCESSIVE DELEGATION

At the other end of the spectrum, are the managers who delegate everything – I mean everything.

I knew one such manager who did this, but when he assigned someone to a project, he wouldn't provide any information. His favorite line was, "Figure it out."

That situation can cause a great deal of stress on the employee and they might spend an inordinate amount of time trying to complete an assignment. They may also be too intimidated to ask for help.

You should always set staff up for success, not failure. This means they understand they can do the job, know what the results and priorities are, and have the appropriate background and training. For you, it means hiring the right staff.

There is a balance between getting rid of the monkey and telling everyone to figure it out.

GUILT COMPLEX

On the more psychological side of things, I've talked with several managers who experience guilt that they passed an assignment on to an employee instead of completing it themselves.

In most cases, this is a fallacy.

I have worked with managers who are very talented but fail to delegate, simply out of guilt.

These are usually good people who just don't realize they are wasting time that could be better spent on other management priorities. Moreover, they are failing to maximize opportunities for the team to contribute and do what they're good at. It also tends to stifle creativity.

One example: When traveling with the government, each traveler must have a Travel Authorization (TA) document that is signed by an official.

One time, I walked into a manager's office and saw her struggling with the preparation of her own TA.

She looked at me and said, "Don't you hate doing these?"

I replied that I had never done one.

She looked surprised.

I told her, "I have one of the staff assistants prepare my TAs."

She responded that she hated to ask someone to do something she could do herself.

We talked a little about all the priorities she had—and she had a lot of them—and it became clear to her that an administrative staff could finish the task in a fraction of the time it was taking her. She finally realized the benefits of appropriate delegation and there was nothing to feel guilty about.

EFFECTIVE DELEGATION

It takes practice identifying what and how to delegate. You must stop and think about this from time to time. Maybe you'll find tasks that would be better delegated. Maybe you should try this with your kids. Here are some questions to consider:

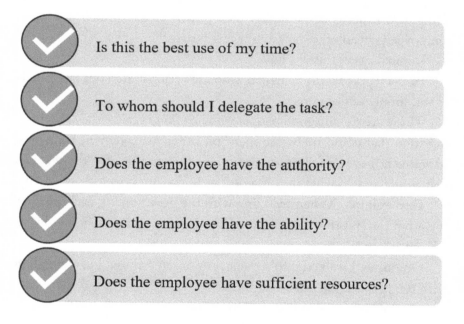

Is this the best use of my time?

To whom should I delegate the task?

Does the employee have the authority?

Does the employee have the ability?

Does the employee have sufficient resources?

DELEGATION CHART

1) Is this a good use of my time? Or are there other more important things that need my attention?
2) To whom should I delegate? For this, you need to know the roles and abilities of each employee.

3) Does the staff member have the authority to complete the task? Unless there is a valid reason, be careful about delegating to someone who is operating outside of his or her position.

4) Does the staff member have the ability to complete the task? Or will delegating the responsibility set someone up for failure? As you get to know your employees, you should have a sense of their abilities, and delegate accordingly.

5) Does the staff member have sufficient resources to complete the task? Resources are vital to the success of the delegated assignment. You can't go to Mars without a spacecraft.

There are times when managers may complete tasks below their pay grade to set an example of "servant leadership," but generally speaking, this reasoning is not sound.

This may sound harsh, but a manager with an annual salary over fifty thousand dollars shouldn't be licking stamps and addressing envelopes. It's just reality.

There are so many things that you should be doing, including budget acquisition, long-range planning, encouraging and coaching other managers and staff, and completing various other high-level tasks. That's why you got promoted to manager. If you feel guilty about that, get over it!

When things are running at their best, everyone is doing their highest value work, and you are making sure the monkeys on your back belong to you. You trust your team, and they get the job done.

With all that said, you can see how delegation both takes practice, and ties in with the other skills of management and leadership—knowing how to decide, how to prioritize, and hiring the right people.

DL #60: If you don't learn the art of delegation, you will constantly have monkeys on your back that don't belong to you.

CHAPTER 9: MAKING EFFECTIVE DECISIONS

LESSON 11

DECIDE TO DECIDE

As a manager, you are going to be making decision after decision after decision. And the higher you climb, the more impact your decisions will have on the whole organization.

Some decisions require an immediate response, where you must trust your gut. Other decisions might not be as urgent, you may have time to analyze, collaborate, and cautiously make those decisions.

Here's an example of a broader decision I had to make last year.

We desperately needed an additional IT Specialist, but I was told the only possible chance to get an additional position was to consolidate our IT department with the Office of Technology at headquarters in DC.

Since I had some time to decide, I wanted to dissect every possible scenario. I started with the traditional pros and cons. After that, I had conversations with our agency chief and our branch chiefs, to discuss all of the possible scenarios. Together, we developed an extensive list of questions for the DC tech office, and then had several in-depth conversations with their office chief.

I also interviewed a manager from another branch office who had recently consolidated with DC, to determine their satisfaction with the centralized approach, and we reviewed analytical data regarding the potential IT security issues if we didn't consolidate.

After gathering all of the information and engaging in more deliberation, the decision was made to centralize. To assure our satisfaction, we drafted a Memorandum of Understanding (MOU).

While there were some challenges at first, we got an additional full-time employee and gradually we learned to navigate with headquarters to improve our technology department. The centralized approach ended up reaping numerous dividends.

As soon as we had our first setback, however, some of the other managers started second-guessing the decision to consolidate.

Stop!

Second guessing every decision is a waste of valuable time. Stop being reactive and start being proactive!

In this case there was an MOU in place and there was no turning back. Once a major decision has been made, seek ways to make it better, but stop second-guessing your decision.

When we overthink a decision, whether through self-doubt, emotions, or some other reason, we exacerbate indecisiveness.

Some decisions are obvious. Call the fire department if your house is on fire, spring into action if you see someone hurting a child. We all get that. Yet, many people struggle with making basic decisions.

Fortunately, years before the IT centralization decision was made, I developed a decision-making process (DMP) to serve as a guide to enhance my own ability to make effective decisions and to minimize the worry of making the wrong decision.

Let's start by exploring how you make decisions with a simple exercise.

There are generally four accepted types of decision-making: Directive, Behavioral, Analytical, and Conceptual. Since Conceptual is used more for long-term concepts, we'll leave that out for purposes of this process. The following scenario will explore Directive, Behavioral, and Analytical.

SCENARIO

You're at a restaurant with a group of colleagues. The waiter brings the food for the entire group, but your entrée is cold.

Generally speaking, do you:

(A) send it back to be heated

(B) talk with others in the group and try to get a consensus about whether you should send it back

(C) take some time to think about the pros and cons of sending it back, including the things that could go wrong

Now, most effective leaders possess some aspects of all of these styles. So, with things having larger stakes, the decision may depend upon the seriousness of the situation, moral beliefs, or the priority level.

But with this simple example, if you said (A) send the food back, your style is Directive. If you said (B) discuss the issue and get feedback from the table, your style is Behavioral. And if you said (C) think and worry about what could go wrong, your default style is Analytical.

Let's look at characteristics of each of these three styles, so you can understand how you're currently making decisions and how you can improve your DMP.

DIRECTIVE STYLE

If your answer was A and you would send the food back, you're probably more aligned with the Directive decision-making process, which is very effective when a short-term decision is needed. The A style leader knows she's hungry and uses her knowledge and experience to make a decision. She sends the food back to be heated. This can be known as experiential or trusting your gut. It can be very effective but has its limitations.

For example, Joan, a manager friend of mine, was very decisive. The problem was that sometimes she made decisions that caused problems for the agency. In one instance, an IT person met with Joan and showed her a new software program that had better graphics. Joan was excited when she saw the demonstration, so she directed procurement to buy thirty licenses for the product.

Sounds great, right?

Well, when the software arrived, it turned out it was incompatible with the current operating system. This caused a great deal of unnecessary work, and a lot of money was wasted, all because Joan jumped the gun too quickly.

The effective Directive leader understands that to keep the organization progressing, tough decisions must be made. In situations that occur instantaneously and require an immediate decision, the Directive manager can quickly choose a direction, communicate that direction, and support and motivate people to achieve results.

The dirty part of Directive leadership is that the Directive leaders will make more mistakes, may take unnecessary risks, and may be prone to making emotional decisions. In addition, some employees may not appreciate the Directive leader's...well, directness. Morale might decline if you're not careful.

In instances when time permits, some Behavioral (B) and Analytical (C) decision-making is required to keep the Directive (A) leader from making hasty, ill-informed decisions.

Back to the restaurant scenario. This situation calls for a quick decision. Therefore, the effective Directive leader is not only decisive, she provides an opportunity for the chef to improve the product— sending the entrée back to be warmed.

DL #61: There are leaders who are decisive and use their past experiences and their guts to make decisions. While this may be effective, when possible they should seek counsel and review data to reach a positive outcome. If there is no time, roll on!

TABLE 1
DIRECTIVE STYLE OF DECISION MAKING

Pros	Cons	Call-To-Action
Decisive.	May be too direct	Must develop a system to know when to collaborate and whether more analytical information is needed
Strong at making short-term decisions	May not be sensitive to staff morale	
Results driven	May not collaborate	
Usually gives clear directives	More prone to making emotional decisions	Consider the impact on staff
Keeps agency moving forward	May make rash decisions	Seek expert opinions
	Will most likely make more mistakes	Use pleasantries when delivering the message

BEHAVIORAL STYLE

If your answer was (B), you may align more with the Behavioral decision-making process. The Behavioral style manager is a good collaborator and would rather make decisions based on a majority opinion.

If you've watched the show, *Who Wants to Be a Millionaire*, contestants are permitted to have a lifeline which allows them to poll the audience. It turns out the audience members are correct nearly every time.

Conversely, when a manager is overly cautious and spends too much time trying to get a consensus, he can cause an organization to become stagnant, and waste time that could have been used in a more productive way.

I once worked with a manager who always wanted to be the center of attention. He loved to be around people and had a great personality. But I noticed he couldn't even go to lunch by himself and would pressure staff to go along with him.

Unfortunately, he took the same approach to making decisions. Not only did he want everyone to agree, he would prolong meetings to try and get a consensus. His staff got so frustrated they would eventually agree with his position just to end the meeting.

The Behavioral decision-maker must understand that there will be times when he can't please everyone and may have to go against the grain. In some instances, he must be straightforward and convey information that might be challenging for others to hear. He may have to enforce policies, make sure deadlines are met, deliver bad news, or administer a personnel action.

If struggling with those cases, the Behavioral manager would need to add some Directive (A) and Analytical (C) style to his repertoire. Without proper development, the lack of decision-making will inevitably permeate the organization and create a whole host of problems.

To be frank, if a primarily Behavioral manager doesn't take affirmative steps to make decisions, he should not seek a higher-level management position. It's easy to get stuck being just a sidekick with little senior management responsibility if you don't add some Directive to your game with practice. Or, enjoy the cold food.

DL #62: There will be times when there won't be a consensus. Stop trying to please everyone and make a decision. Get acquainted with your gut. Hopefully, it will lead you in the right direction.

TABLE 2
BEHAVIORAL STYLE OF DECISION MAKING

Pros	Cons	Call-To-Action
Good collaborator	May be timid	Start making quick decisions when needed, based on experience and gut instinct
Desires a majority opinion in making decisions	Struggles when quick decisions are needed	
Won't make hasty decisions	Decisions may cause internal stress	Think of the organizational needs first and accept the fact that it is impossible to please everyone
Considers staff morale	Focuses on others' reactions before making a decision	
	May wait too long to make a decision	Must overcome the psychological need to be loved
		Consensus or not, make a decision

ANALYTICAL STYLE

If you answered (C), you probably relate more to the Analytical decision-making process. The Analytical style manager wants all of the facts, the pros and cons, and any other data that is available before making a decision.

The Analytical manager is likely to make solid decisions, but it may take more time.

This style is very effective when careful consideration is warranted, but other times you must be decisive quickly without all of the facts. This can be a challenge for the Analytical type manager, and you may benefit from practice, starting with small situations like the cold meal scenario. Identify those and practice being decisive.

Likewise, Analytical managers should develop an explicit prioritization process to know when collaboration B-style is needed or when an immediate decision A-style must be made.

If you're Analytical by default, be careful you don't let the pursuit of perfection prevent you from getting things done on time. I knew a manager who couldn't finish reports in a timely manner because he kept searching for more and more information, believing that the reports were incomplete. He kept missing deadlines, and even after being cautioned about this, he couldn't get things done by the deadline. Ultimately, he left that job. Having an explicit prioritization process and practicing making fast decisions can help prevent this from happening to you.

If you relate to Analytical style, you must practice making quicker decisions in the smaller areas. Don't worry so much about minutia. You'll discover that you're right more often than you think. If others in your party have finished eating and you're still trying to make a decision about whether to send the food back, you've probably waited too long.

DL #63: Data is paramount in today's world of evidence-based outcomes. Nonetheless, as a manager, you have to be able to make quick decisions based on your experience. If the light is red, there's no time for data. Just stop the car.

TABLE 3

ANALYTICAL STYLE OF DECISION MAKING

Pros	Cons	Call-To-Action
Data driven Makes evidence-based decisions Perfectionist Considers variables Outcome driven Often makes the right decision	Has trouble making quick decisions Struggles making decisions without significant data May waste valuable time May accept data despite employee morale	Must practice making some decisions based on experience and gut Consider both employee morale and data when making decisions Recognize that perfection isn't always attainable

As with all things, start by understanding where you are, and then practice.

All effective leaders and managers learn their strengths and weaknesses, and look to incorporate the best elements of different decision-making styles over time. Make time to practice this since it will serve you your whole life.

CHAPTER 10: STANDARDS

LESSON III

NO STANDARDS

I have this buddy, we'll call him Devon, who was always going on dating sites. He said he was ready to settle down if he could meet the right girl. Yet, every time I asked him how his dating life was going, he would drop his head and say, "It's terrible." I would always ask why. He recounted one nightmare story after another.

The two that stand out the most for me were Debbie and Monica. Date #1: Debbie.

Devon and Debbi started corresponding on the dating app and wanted to arrange to meet but kept having scheduling conflicts. Finally, Debbie told Devon just to stop by and say hello on his way home from work. He said he gave her an estimated time and texted to let her know he had arrived.

He rang the doorbell and she came to the door almost immediately. He described her as attractive and pleasant. Then he paused. "Okay, what happened next?" I asked.

Before she invited him in, she said, "Excuse the mess." Then he followed her inside. He said when he saw her apartment, the only relatable description he could conjure up in his mind was "crime scene."

Devon said trash, boxes, dirty dishes, and cat hair were everywhere. There were clothes strewn on the floor, the table, and the couch.

She asked him to have a seat. He replied, "Where should I sit?" She said, "The couch is fine." He moved some things out of the way and took a seat. Just then, one of her four cats jumped on his lap.

At his point, he was freaking out. He asked her if she was moving or something. She said no, she had just been a little busy. Finally, he semi-jokingly—okay, he wasn't joking—asked if she had ever considered being on the TV show, *Hoarders*.

She didn't think that was funny, so the meet and greet ended soon after.

The funniest part was that he just couldn't stop describing her apartment. Every time we got together, he recalled a few more items he had forgotten to tell me about.

Date #2: Monica. Circa two weeks after Debbie.

A few weeks later, Devon and I met for lunch. Of course, I couldn't help but ask how his quest for Mrs. Right was going. He then started telling me about Monica. Much like Debbie, he and Monica had been texting through an app. They set a time and place to meet.

They met at a local restaurant and she was sitting at the bar. She greeted him with a hug, and they took a seat. He described Monica in much the same way as Debbie. Attractive and pleasant.

She was easy to talk to, and things seemed to be going well. He even fought off the urge to ask her thoughts on cleanliness and organization. Then they discussed the challenges of dating, schedules, children, careers, etc.

Monica said, "Imagine how hard it is for me!"

Devon was confused.

He said, "What do you mean?" She replied, "Well some people are uncomfortable when they meet my husband."

Devon was stunned. He said, "What?! Your husband?" She said "Yes. He'll be joining us in a bit."

Devon was shocked!

He politely explained that he hadn't realized she was married, and certainly didn't know her husband would be joining them. She replied, "Didn't you read my profile?" Devon had not. He apologized for the misunderstanding and left.

At that point, I scolded him a little for not reading her profile. He didn't laugh but told me he was so busy he usually just scrolled through the pictures.

Then he dropped his head and said he didn't think he would ever meet someone who didn't have major issues.

That gave me an idea.

I asked, "What does your profile say?" To my surprise, he said, "Hold on and I'll show you."

He pulled out his phone and held it up where I could read.

His profile literally said, "Wanting to meet women nearby. Good job. Too busy to drive more than ten miles."

I said, "Know why you're having so much trouble? You have no standards."

BASIC STANDARDS

Let's get serious. The word standards can have a lot of meanings. There are high standards, low standards, double standards, and no standards.

What comes to mind when you hear someone say, "That restaurant has high standards?" You probably think the restaurant is clean, the staff is professional, and the food is of high quality.

Standards can determine if your company succeeds or fails.

A standard is usually established by consensus and provides rules, guidelines, or characteristics for activities that your company plans to align itself with. Without standards, your business will fail to evolve and start to deteriorate. Basically, standards are a reflection of what is important to you and your company.

LOW STANDARDS

In 2016, I moved into a new apartment complex with my daughter, Jansen, for a brief period.

This place had high standards. Everything was well-kept. The landscaping was manicured, the pool was well maintained, the outside propane tanks were always full, and the list goes on and on. After about ten months, I received a notice that a different company had purchased the complex.

Soon after, things began to deteriorate.

The landscaping started to look unkempt, there was trash laying around, and I went down to use the barbeque and the tanks were empty. I knew someone who worked in the main office and questioned her about what was going on.

She said the new company had reduced the services to save money. Basically, they had lowered their standards.

As soon as my lease expired, I moved. Several other tenants did the same.

Never settle for low standards – if that's what you offer, that's what you'll get.

STANDARDS = IMPROVEMENT

I have mentioned that I had the honor of being on the Federal Law Enforcement Training Accreditation Board, including serving as its chair from 2012 to 2014. Accreditation is made up of agreed-upon standards that federal law enforcement academies and training programs must adhere to in order to be accredited. These standards ensure that training operates with fidelity and professionalism. They cover everything from record keeping to confidentiality to quality training.

In order to be accredited, your program must pass an assessment by a team made up of various federal law enforcement agencies. The process is rigorous but has elevated the quality of training throughout the United States.

You should make sure your company has high standards and be willing to have someone review them for quality from time to time.

In developing standards, a good guide is the military mantra, "People first, mission always."

If you want your organization and team to flourish, you must find the balance between caring for staff and carrying out the mission. You know you have the right standards when the two align.

Taking care of staff should be at the top of your list. When you display interest, empathy, and concern for your team, they will follow you to the ends of the earth.

As a result, the mission will most certainly be completed with passion and fortitude. Whether that's sales, law enforcement, or moving furniture across the country in an eighteen-wheeler.

Here are just a few examples of standards:

Employee satisfaction: We will provide avenues for employees to provide input on job satisfaction with a view toward improving the employee morale and resources.

Continuing employee development: We will strive to provide employees with the resources to obtain training, the equipment to enhance their knowledge, and to make sure they are evolving to meet their objectives.

Customer service: We strive to give our customers the best service possible and to make sure they are satisfied with their experience.

Innovation: We will remain on the cutting edge of innovation through research of evidence-based practices, technology, and employee development.

Quality control: We will develop a system of maintaining the standards of our products and services by testing samples of the output against the specifications.

High Standards will serve to enhance your brand and help the agency or company in all parts of the business.

> DL #64: The highest standard is maintaining healthy staff and promoting a robust mission. When these align, other standards will be easy to implement.

PERSONAL STANDARDS

We've discussed high standards and their importance to your business. However, without personal standards these might be a moot point. Let's do a deep dive into personal standards.

Personal standards are mostly a set of behaviors that we consistently choose to exhibit. They define how we want to treat others and how we want to be treated. In reality, your personal standards are a reflection of your self-esteem. If you have high standards you command respect, but if you have low standards you will likely be disrespected.

If your standards are high, it doesn't mean you're arrogant, it simply means you have confidence. By setting standards, there are intrinsic lines you don't cross. Your personal standards are also evidenced by the promises you keep, in the way you dress and manage your life, health, finances, etc.

Most people form a first impression of you within thirty to sixty seconds. Depending on your demeanor, eye contact, words, dress, and many other factors, others can usually tell if you are a person with high or low standards.

Adapting high standards into your life will enhance your work, family, and nearly every part of your life.

Maintaining high standards takes decisive action. If you have not thought about your personal standards in some time, start with a piece of paper and make three columns.

On the first column write Standards. In the next one, write Barriers and on the third, write Call to Action.

For example, you might want to become more proactive. The Standard would be "Proactive." The Barriers might be "self-doubt/

previous failure." The Call to Action might be "Set hourly goals, tasks/to do list, note progress.

This is a simple exercise but an important one.

STANDARDS	BARRIERS	CALL TO ACTION
° PROACTIVE	° SELF DOUBT	° SET HOURLY GOALS
	° PREVIOUS FAILURE	° TASKS / TO DO LIST
		° NOTE PROGRESS

DL #65: Unfortunately, there are managers who have poor standards and model behavior that is beneath their company's mission, and that behavior permeates throughout the organization. Leaders must set the tone.

CHAPTER 11: ROLE CLARIFICATION

LESSON IV

Ambiguity with roles, responsibilities and company policy tends to lead to poor productivity, and leaves managers and staff feeling confused and miserable.

But seriously, it's a headache when you don't have this situation under control. And most organizations don't. As a manager you must understand your role in your organization, yes, but also the roles of other managers and your staff. Then you've got to get everyone working together.

To become dialed-in as a great team, everyone needs to know what their job is and what it isn't.

Most managers just accept a ton of ambiguity and feel it's simply the way things are. Let's fight that together.

WHAT CITY ARE THOSE COOKIES IN?

As academy director, I was based in Charleston, South Carolina, but our headquarters was in Washington, D.C. There was a central email loop that I received, but many of the messages in it were only relevant to the DC office. You've got to be ready for this as a manager. You're going to get voluminous amounts of emails and other communications that have little, if anything, to do with your responsibilities. And you'll receive more of it the more senior you get.

If you're not careful, this flood of information will suppress your level of output and that of colleagues and team members—both those who report to you, and those who don't.

In a particularly funny moment, I kept getting emails noting there were cookies at the end of the hallway. I looked for the cookies in Charleston a couple times. Never found them. Finally, when I visited headquarters, I was with John Hughes, the head of our system at that time, and we were walking around the office. Suddenly, at the end of the hallway, I saw the cookies.

I blurted out, "I've been looking for these darn cookies for months, and I finally found them!"

John and I had a good laugh, but I think I made the point that I was forced to wade through numerous irrelevant emails on a daily basis.

It's easy for people to become overwhelmed with information that isn't relevant to them or their responsibilities. It's part of your job as a manager to minimize the amount of clutter going out to people, in order to ensure they pay close attention to what is relevant. Hint: Don't Reply to All if it doesn't apply to All.

AMBIGUITY IS THE ENEMY

I repeat: Roles within an organization must be clarified to move the needle forward. Ambiguity must be identified as a problem.

There are many possible culprits that can add to confusion and a lack of clarity.

For instance:

- Poorly written job descriptions that are generic in nature.
- A failure to clarify roles and responsibilities.
- Poor communication from management.
- Failure to develop and introduce all staff to the organization's policies, procedures, and processes.

The above are not all inclusive, there may be many more.

If someone's job description is generic and unclear, rewrite it. You can include that person in the re-write to make sure it accurate. If it's not clear who is responsible for a given activity, work it out. If two people both think it's their job, get together with them and clarify their roles and responsibilities.

Ambiguity means time lost and frustration from staff and stakeholders.

True leaders make sure their employees are not wandering around in the dark. They shine a bright light in every nook and cranny for everyone to see. Hunt out ambiguity and clarify it. It might seem daunting at first but doing so makes everyone's job much clearer and more enjoyable.

OVERLAPPING RESPONSIBILITIES

There are positions in most organizations that overlap. In some situations, the person with the strongest personality will attempt to pass duties off to the weaker staff member or takeover the duties if they get recognition.

As a manager, I had two staff members with similar responsibilities. Staff member one, in an attempt to avoid a task, would say that the particular assignment should be completed by staff member two. Unfortunately, staff member two would usually take the assignment simply to avoid conflict.

When this was brought to my attention, I intervened and assigned tasks accordingly.

This situation is not always black and white and requires managers to balance the mission with individual workloads.

You should look to balance your assessment between the most skilled person to complete the task and the current workload distribution and assign tasks accordingly.

While there will always be some gray areas, don't allow employees to default to "That's not my responsibility." If the job descriptions or policies are unclear, change them.

DL #66: Managers must understand their roles and the roles of their staff, the proper chain of command, and the sufficient amount of information distributed to make sure time is not wasted.

CHAPTER 12: EFFECTIVE COMMUNICATION

LESSON V

Isn't it interesting how communication and communication skills have probably been addressed more than any topic, yet there are numerous organizations who continue to have major communication problems?

I remember when I attended my first meeting at the Federal Law Enforcement Training Center. I was really excited. But my excitement waned a little when the first presenter spoke for eleven minutes and managed to use over twenty acronyms during that time.

I only knew what three of them meant.

Was that good communication?

As a manager, a huge part of your job is communicating. But a lot of people get confused as to what communication is.

I've found that nearly all problems that occur in the workplace can be attributed to the poor exchange of information. So, let's look at some key aspects of communication and how your communications will impact your time, efforts, and results.

Then, we'll discuss some ways to improve.

COMMUNICATION STYLES TO AVOID

Do you ever talk with someone and you're just not sure what they're trying to say?

Let's take a humorous look at some communication styles to avoid.

You shouldn't feel bad if you're not perfect; nobody is. We've all got to improve. So, think for a moment if you're communicating any of these styles:

Indirect Communicator: Brandy liked to communicate with metaphors. For example, when an employee asked a question, she would respond, "If you push the right button, the elevator stops at the correct floor." Or, "Flowers only bloom in the spring." She loved her metaphors, and they were often quite funny. The problem was that staff often left her office confused.

Passive Aggressive Communicator: Jack used sarcasm to make a point. If he wasn't pleased with someone's work, he would tell them, "Some employees catch on quicker than others." Or, "If this were surgery, you would have cut off his ear." This type of communication also breeds confusion, but defensiveness and hostility too. Remember, it's not always what is said, but what is heard.

Generic Communicator: Then there was Wayne who sent generic emails to make a point, instead of talking to the individual who needed the information. Once, an employee came in late on several occasions and, instead of addressing the behavior with the employee, this manager sent an email to everyone that said tardiness was unacceptable, leaving most of the employees confused. Just like the other types of communication above, this communication was left to interpretation.

Non-Communicator: Early in my career, I received an email from Walt, a senior executive, advising that we were going to get new computers. We waited for about two weeks and heard nothing else on the topic. I approached one of the supervisors and asked about the new computers. I mentioned that Walt had told me he would let me know when my computer arrived. I told the supervisor that other staff in his unit were also asking the same question. He replied, "Let them know they will get them when they get them." Now that was solid communication! He also made me his press secretary to deliver his response to the masses.

Rambling Communicator: Doug usually said a lot without saying anything. He would just ramble on and on, and never really make a point. One day Doug was leading a meeting in the conference room on whether to reclassify two positions to better meet the needs of the agency. Seemed like a good topic. Right? We started the meeting at 9:00 a.m., and after about an hour and a half we still hadn't really discussed the reasons to reclassify the positions. Doug kept throwing out ideas and went on and on about the history of the company. He talked about the old days and how they used to do things. Suddenly Mike, an employee who was known to be quite assertive, blurted out, "What the hell are you talking about and how does this relate to reclassifying positions?" Of course, Mike said what we were all thinking. Doug glared at him looking very irate, and we all thought, "This is it, Mike's going to get canned." However, after staring at Mike for a few seconds, Doug finally got to the point.

You spot any of yourself in those styles? As with all management and leadership skills, we can work on –our communication, but it starts with being honest with yourself. If you're being Indirect, Passive Aggressive, Non-Communicating, or Rambling, simply recognize it and then get to work to improve.

While it's funny to read these examples, we all know these styles aren't effective, and yet we've all experienced at least some of them. Why does that happen?

ASSERTIVENESS AND FEAR

Excluding Doug, the rambling manager, the root of most of these styles of communication is fear. People are afraid to express their true intent, so they mask their words to provide some level of protection.

It is one thing to know how to communicate but a whole different animal to deliver the truth, particularly when the message might be unpopular.

In the years I experienced bullying, one guy called me a bunch of nasty names in front of some other kids. I was so angry, I thought I was going to explode.

I knew exactly what I wanted to say, I just didn't have the cajones to say it.

When I got home, I stood in front of a mirror and reenacted the event.

I was so tough in the mirror!

The problem was the disappointment I experienced for feeling like a coward.

The courage to communicate clearly and precisely produces inner peace.

On an old TV series called Billy Jack, the protagonist - Billy Jack - was a karate expert. On one show, he looks a guy right in the eye and says, "I'm going take this right foot, and I'm gonna whop you on that side of your face." Billy even pointed to the exact spot. Then he did it.

Whop!

Now, that's straightforward communication. It validated the old adage, "Say what you mean and mean what you say."

There are times when managers must be assertive and direct. While you don't want to be rude, direct communication—including empathy where needed—will improve nearly every aspect of your life. As a byproduct, good communication skills will minimize stress for you and your team.

If you struggle with assertiveness, start practicing direct communication in simple conversations. "No, I don't enjoy that." "Please complete the assignment by noon tomorrow." "Please don't lecture me every time I ask a question." Over time, your courage will increase, and you and your staff will perform more expeditiously.

AN EASY WAY TO START PRACTICING COMMUNICATION

One of the best ways to improve communication is to practice. One way is to script your message and read it to yourself. This will improve fluency with the message.

You've got opportunities to practice all the time. As you converse with someone, be cognizant of your words. Be clear and concise, and make sure you're understood. Think about what you want to convey.

Do you want to emphasize a point? Ask for a favor? Or, give an assignment?

Each must be delivered with clarity but might require more emphasis.

Let's say you just ate at a new restaurant and were very impressed. You have a good friend who is a food connoisseur and loves to try new places to eat.

As funny as this might sound, you can use this as a low-stakes opportunity to practice. Let's say you're a little shy and indirect. In this situation, you could try being more emphatic. "You have to try this new restaurant!" Sounds simple but try it.

Likewise, if you felt your communication was a little too bland, you could try using more persuasive and evocative words. "The food is delicious, the service is impeccable, and the atmosphere is very vibrant and lively."

When you spot a gap in your communication style, you can practice filling it. Pick a point of emphasis and work on it, and it will carry forward into all your communication.

CLARITY AND DIRECTNESS

As you manage more people and responsibilities over time, you need to make sure your communication is becoming clearer and more direct. Little instances of being unclear or indirect can waste a whole lot of time.

Let's say you want to meet your friend Melinda for lunch, so you send her a text message that says, "Do you want to meet downtown for lunch?" This will likely start a series of back and forth texts that might take more time than the lunch itself.

Now, let's rephrase the text to Melinda in a more direct, clear, concise manner. "Do you want to meet at Alamo Barbeque downtown at noon for lunch?"

While the second text might not be as collaborative, in most cases it will garner a more direct response.

In other words, Melinda will tend to follow suit with your direct communication. She might respond, "I had barbeque yesterday. How about Sebastiano's Italian restaurant at noon?"

Done.

In a business setting, I have seen managers waste an inordinate amount of time by failing to be direct and concise in their communication.

Here another example, once, I was on an email thread where a manager wanted to schedule a meeting. He sent an email to five employees and me.

The email read, "Can you all meet tomorrow?"

There were five different responses.

Employee 1: "What time?"

Employee 2: "I have a one o'clock, otherwise free."

Employee 3: "I am tied up most of the morning. Can we do it in the afternoon?"

Employee 4: "My schedule is pretty good; except I have a Zoom meeting at nine o'clock."

Employee 5: "I have several meetings. What are we discussing and how long will the meeting last?"

I certainly wasn't going to confuse this situation further, so I called the manager. I determined the reason for the meeting and suggested that staff tend to be free first thing in the morning or toward the end of the day. I said just send an invite that explains the meeting topic and set it for 8:00 a.m. Everyone accepted the meeting invite.

While it might require some adjustments to get one hundred percent attendance, when you communicate clearly the purpose, location, a suggested time, and length of the meeting, you will usually save time and effort. If everyone can't attend, determine which staff members are more vital to the meeting and work around their schedules. You can share the meeting notes or brief the other staff members as soon as possible. All part of good communication.

MEMORABLE COMMUNICATION

Have you ever had someone say something to you that you never forgot? Something that was so powerful it left an indelible mark in your memory.

While most people think this ability is something you're just born with, but it can be learned and practiced.

Leaders are in a position to mentor and influence their staff members and have a profound impact on their future. I can still remember certain actions or statements that leaders or managers made to me that turned out to be defining moments in my life.

One particular moment that had an impact on me occurred just after I had been selected as academy director. The previous academy director, Sharon, had a few more days left before retirement, so we met to help me prepare for the job.

Sharon gave me some of that "table talk," the really valuable stuff that's usually learned more informally. I'll never forget Sharon telling me, "Don't try to solve everyone's problems. Some people just want to be heard."

To be honest, at the time it made sense, but it didn't seem to be anything profound.

Nonetheless, as I matured into the position, I realized how powerful her advice really was, and I never forgot it.

When you hear communication like that, don't just appreciate it, think it through and try to understand why it had such an influence on you.

Also, at some point you'll find yourself saying something that really leaves a mark on one of your staff. When that happens, don't just appreciate it. Make time to think about why it made such a big difference.

Over time, you can identify what really moves you, and when you're making a huge mark. You can practice doing more of that over time, and it's beautiful when you can help someone make a permanent change with an unforgettable and profound statement or question.

COMMUNICATION THROUGH ACTION

My supervisor in DC, Nancy Beatty, had a profound impact on me through her actions. There were so many difficult issues that we faced together.

But no matter the situation, she would always begin the conversation with a pleasant greeting and, at some point, say something funny to lighten the mood.

Once we were talking about budget cuts which could lead to layoffs. The conversation was grim. Out of nowhere, Nancy exclaimed, "See, I told you I would give you a vacation!" We had a much-needed laugh. It was always like that with Nancy: she was one of the most optimistic and consistent leaders I have ever worked with.

Gene DiMaria another manager I worked with, was punctual, organized, and passionate about the mission. He was always at work on time or early, and completed assignments ahead of schedule. Gene set an example through his actions.

Often, if an employee arrived late, they would head straight to Gene's office to explain. He hadn't said a word.

Get it?

He wasn't a micro manager, he communicated by example.

PAYING ATTENTION

An important aspect of communication is listening to understand.

One day, I was having lunch with my youngest daughter, Jansen, and she was sharing a story with me. At some point I started looking at my phone, and in a very direct tone she said, "Please don't look at your phone while I'm talking to you." Lesson learned.

At work, I had a senior manager visit me once from headquarters, and he kept looking at his watch while I was talking. Of course, I shut down like congress before a holiday.

I think you're getting the point. If you truly want to be a good communicator, give individuals your undivided attention. And you should not only gather details, but also listen for subtle cues. The person might be letting you know they are in pain or distressed. This is often referred to as "active listening."

It's a good idea in some instances to reiterate parts of a conversation, to make sure you both have the same understanding.

ONE LINE ZINGERS

I absolutely love to watch political debates. The information exchange is quite interesting. It's amazing when a debater makes that one comment that everyone knows is a homerun.

In 1984, Ronald Reagan was running for reelection. He was the oldest president in the history of the country. He was debating Walter Mondale, and since there were rumors floating around about Reagan's mental faculties, he was asked a question about his age. Reagan replied, "I want you to know I will not make age an issue in this campaign. I am not going to exploit for political purposes my opponent's youth and inexperience." That response is still talked about to this day.

It is doubtful that the one-line zingers are organic. They are probably rehearsed, and the debater is praying for an opening to use that special phrase. If you're serious about improving, take the necessary steps to make your communication meaningful.

Years ago, I worked with a colleague who was very positive. Toward the end of the day, he would ask, "Did you conquer the day?" Although I had to think about that one, I quickly realized he was asking if I had accomplished great things. Sometimes he would just look at me, and I'd say, "Yes I conquered the day."

HUMOR

Humor can diffuse a tense situation, or simply engage the listener. When done appropriately, it can make communication more effective.

Once I took a team to conduct an audit of a U.S. probation office in the northeast part of the country. The review team found some errors with the substance abuse contracting. During the daily debriefing, one of my team members leading that part of the audit met with the office's substance abuse contract specialist to address an issue.

As the conversation progressed, the contract specialist got very defensive and became angry. Things started to escalate, so I knew I had to do something.

I loudly interjected that all this talk about substance abuse had made me thirsty, so let's end for the day and get a drink! There were a couple of chuckles in the room and the tension was reduced.

As we walked out, I smiled at the contract specialist and said, "We may determine there are some issues with the way you do contracting, but we certainly will not question your passion for the job." She actually mustered a slight smile. We concluded the meeting and resumed the following morning. After a good night's sleep, the meeting went much better.

There are other great examples of humor being used to deescalate a situation.

When John F. Kennedy appointed his brother Bobby to be attorney general amid calls of nepotism, he replied, "I see nothing wrong with giving Robert some legal experience as attorney general before he goes out to practice law." After reporters had a good laugh, the topic was rarely visited again.

But humor can also be a career ender. Always avoid major topics such as sex or sexual innuendo, race, religion, politics, weight, disabilities, social judgments, singling out any particular group, and the list goes on. While this list isn't designed to stifle your creative humor, you must be cautious. It is also vital to know your audience before any attempts at humor.

PRACTICE, PRACTICE, PRACTICE

A lot of people seem to believe humor, poise, and clarity are something you're born with, something you either have or don't have. I hope you're starting to see that's untrue.

You can work on practicing your communication in a variety of situations. Start with small stuff, from being clearer about a lunch meeting to recommending a restaurant. From there, work on improving your communication with your team, superiors, and stakeholders.

The nice thing is, all these skills work together. Defining roles clearly makes it easier to communicate. Understanding how you make decisions lets you learn what situations you have to be careful in, and how to expand the way you think. Delegating correctly and getting the monkey off your back gives you more time to set high standards and gives you more time to practice being a better leader and manager.

As you practice each one of these five core skills, doing so makes all the rest of them easier, and you're on the way to managing and leading a great team in an environment that could be called a well-oiled machine.

DL #67 Effective communication is the backbone of any business. Without courage, communication will always be tainted.

PART III

FUNDAMENTAL PRINCIPLES

I want to talk with you about some foundational principles to get you off to the right start. These being establishing yourself as a leader, providing staff expectations, spending time with line staff and managers to build trust and understanding, communicating a clear vision, and building a high-performing, positive culture.

If these principles are weak, you're going to find yourself fighting fires and dealing with all sorts of crazy problems in the moment, rather than working to achieve the higher goals. You might not realize these annoying issues are due to missing or weak foundations, but once you get those in place, you'll be amazed at how much smoother things begin to run.

Whenever you're promoted into a new role, whenever things have changed recently, whenever you are growing your team, or if things have seemed crazy of late, it's time to look at the foundations of your management.

It's easy not to realize you're missing these basic foundations, but if things are getting crazy, those are the rocks to turn over and look under.

CHAPTER 13: ESTABLISH YOURSELF AS A LEADER

Difficult question: Why would a fellow manager or staff ever disrespect you?

Actually, the question isn't difficult. The answer is difficult.

Because they think they can.

Look, people are funny. There are some people who are always great at their job, but there are a lot more people who will only perform well for a respected manager.

Almost all of us deal with this issue when we first get promoted.

For me, when I got promoted, I felt the need to display over-dramatized humility, particularly with middle managers, some of whom had also applied for my position. Heck, to be fully honest about it, I almost begged some of them to support me. I'm a bit embarrassed as I write this.

But the managers, the agency, and the staff were looking for a leader. I had to learn to take my place of authority and do it quickly.

You must do the same. I'm not talking arrogance here. I'm talking confidence. Everything from the way you dress to the way you carry yourself, to conveying that you are ready, willing, and able to lead.

But it goes beyond that. It's not just clothes or body language or word choices. It starts in your mind.

Think about a presidential inaugural address. No matter who wins the election, there is one thing that is always clear—the world is watching, and the president always projects leadership.

When a newly elected president speaks, you will never hear statements like, "I can't believe I got this position."

Or, "Not sure how we'll do this year, but we'll try."

No. You will hear strength, solutions, and a call for unity.

Of course, there are realities to face in your organization. And while staff usually already understand the strengths and weaknesses of the organization, you must become the symbol of hope.

Find that balance between confidence and humility. It starts in your mind. You got the job. You have the job because a leader was needed. Remember that.

Model excellence, be responsive to phone calls, emails, text messages, listen to understand, make decisions with confidence, and establish yourself as a leader.

DL #68: If you don't establish your role as the leader, someone else will fill the void and win the influence of staff. Establish credibility right out of the gate.

BASIC EXPECTATIONS

In a perfect world you wouldn't have to provide fundamental expectations.

It's a fact that employees respond better to agreements and shared goals.

The only problem is human behavior.

If you don't lay your foundation of service and expectations from the outset, someone will engage in extreme behavior and afterward try to play ignorant by acting like they didn't realize they'd done anything wrong.

Again, there are a lot of people who will perform well for a leader they respect and with whom they have established a strong foundation.

Others will act in rather surprising ways. You'll deal with a lot of different personalities when you become a manager. Some things may even shock you.

I was once surprised after I got a promotion during my time as a U.S. probation officer. Another officer who had applied for the same position wouldn't speak to me for months. This type of behavior is immature and can leave you wondering if there's something wrong with you.

Well, maybe not. Usually people don't talk very much about this sort of thing, because often when you are new you get embarrassed, but these issues go away once you learn the skills and have the mindset to manage and lead.

Whenever you get a new promotion, you can expect the following reactions:

1) Those who are genuinely happy for you and believe that you were the best candidate.

2) Those who competed for the job but lost. Some will move on, but some may hold a grudge and will want you to fail.

3) The disgruntled people who think they are smarter and cooler than everyone else including you.

4) The neutrals who will give you a chance, but you had better meet their expectations.

Don't let the negatives get in your head or steal your time. In other words, don't major on the minors.

Remember, they either didn't apply for the job or they weren't selected. You were chosen for the role. Own it.

To promote maximum performance, managers should establish agreements with staff on assignments, projects, responsibilities, etc. An agreement and shared goals are very effective in making things run smoothly.

However, there are some basic expectations that are non-negotiable. You might even forget that you need to establish these because they seem like common sense, but even solid teams need a leader to actively reinforce—and if necessary, enforce—the following. You should explicitly set expectations covering such categories as treating others with dignity and respect—the officer who refused to speak with me violated this expectation—teamwork, integrity, a willingness to learn, and a commitment to be a good steward of the organization's resources.

These might sound like basic points, but people appreciate hearing from their manager that they're committed to these principles. People perform better when they know that's also what is expected of them.

Take some time to think about these. Even commit them to paper. Run them by a trusted friend outside the organization for feedback. Your foundational expectations will vary based on your organization, but don't neglect them just because they seem basic.

Once you've done the first round of developing these fundamental expectations, make sure they align with company code of conduct, and policy and procedures. Then, vet them with your superiors and human resources for validation.

While all this might sound like a no-brainer, you'd be surprised by how often this management step gets missed entirely, and what a huge difference it can make.

As you meet with employees to discuss expectations and agreements, be friendly but direct. While other parts of the organization may be fluid, your expectations should be etched in stone. These should align with the organization's vision, policies, and code of conduct—but your expectations should be more specific.

I've found it's best to have all employees sign a document with those expectations outlined and give them a copy. This document conveys in clear and precise terms that you are serious about your position and your pursuit of excellence. You can refer to these expectations when you have personnel issues, and they can serve as a layer of protection to safeguard you from complaints or appeals.

At one point, I had to administer a personnel action and suspended an employee for misuse of electronics. When I took action, the staff expectations document proved beneficial. It served as added authority when the dirty personnel issue surfaced. And trust me, they will surface.

But more than that, these aren't a set of rules. They are the way your team is going to get things done, work together, and treat each other right.

For any younger staff reporting to you, they might never have experienced working under a manager who sets high expectations. You'll hear from them that it's exciting, and it leads to everyone raising the bar, treating each other better, having a more enjoyable and pleasant workplace, and getting a lot more done.

And yeah, I'll say it again. It'll also save you a lot of headaches.

CREATING AN EXPECTATIONS DOCUMENT

As noted, agencies and businesses tend to have codes of conduct or similar requirements. Your expectations document should be more specific to promote excellence and encourage teamwork.

In order to create an expectations document, you must know the organization's values. A simplistic approach to getting started is to envision the model avatar and how they could contribute to the team.

Here are a few starting points for an expectations document:
- Safety
- Integrity
- Teamwork
- Creativity
- Professional Growth
- Handling Company Resources
- Communication
- Initiative

After you make a list of expectations, elaborate on each. The document should be very clear but not written in a way that comes across like a set of rules or as a warning.

Next is a sample Expectations Document.

SAMPLE EXPECTATIONS DOCUMENT FOR PRINT, EDIT AND USE

INTRODUCTION:

The purpose of this document is to state some basic conduct and performance expectations for all staff. The expectations outlined herein are intended to maximize your ability to achieve excellence in all areas of your professional duties, both as an individual and as (Name of company/agency) staff collectively.

EXPECTATIONS:

Safety and Security – All staff must take the necessary steps and precautions to maintain a safe and secure workplace for employees, customers, and internal and external stakeholders at all times. Safety and security matters must be given paramount priority as we perform our duties. (Include applicable safety procedures for your business, e.g., emergency drills.)

Teamwork – Staff is expected to work together in a cooperative and helpful manner and to treat each other with respect and dignity, regardless of race, ethnicity, gender, religious beliefs, or sexual orientation. Teamwork is fostered by staff members who readily and willingly offer assistance to their peers and who honor their own commitments when scheduled to perform a task. You are here to perform very important duties and cannot be distracted by negative influences. Flexibility and a "can do" attitude are major positive factors in promoting harmony and goodwill among all staff.

Communication – Open communication among staff at all levels is vitally important for the proper exchange and dissemination of information and ideas. You are expected to mean what you say and to say what you mean in clear, concise, and respectful terms. All levels of management will have an open-door philosophy and are available to discuss any questions or ideas you have.

Striving for Excellence – During our history, we have established an outstanding reputation for providing high quality (services and products.) Regardless of how well you are performing your duties, you must be open to new ideas and constructive feedback that will promote your continued improvement. Those who are committed to excellence must not only identify and define problems, but they should also offer realistic solutions to each problem when possible.

Information Technology – We will continue to emphasize the use of information technology and advanced communication systems. We are committed to keeping abreast of current and future technology trends in this rapidly changing field. The use of company technological resources is for business-related purposes only.

Responsiveness – Timely and accurate responses to inquiries, letters, emails, calls, texts, etc. are vital to maintaining a credible and efficient (company). Staff must be responsive to each other, colleagues, customers, and internal and external stakeholders.

Accountability – You are the steward of (company/public) funds and must use all resources in a prudent manner. You are accountable for honoring attendance and leave requirements, procurement requirements, and for performing all assigned and related duties. Also, you are accountable for making sound decisions and for making reasonable recommendations.

DL #69: Always pursue shared agreements, and provide staff with clear expectations. Then expect the best but prepare for the worst.

CHAPTER 14: SPEND TIME WITH ALL LEVELS OF EMPLOYEES

Leave the comfort of your office and visit staff.

All levels of staff.

If you're new to the job, set this up as a habit and keep it up. If times have gotten crazy and you've found yourself buried in your office, start reestablishing this as part of your routine. Time block it in your calendar.

When you meet staff at all different levels, they will provide you with helpful information and fresh perspectives you cannot get anywhere else. This will often produce new ideas or specific information that will help with policy and procedure development and promote the right culture.

Once, I was making my rounds and stopped by to check on a new staff member. During the conversation, we discussed the fact that it was difficult for students at the academy to find some of the training venues. Then he hesitated and said, "I know I'm new, but I might have a solution." He suggested monitors throughout the building that listed all the classes and the room number.

I took this idea to the FLETC officials and offered to purchase the monitors. Before long, the monitors were installed and activated, which proved to be a tremendous benefit to the students.

This was all precipitated by spending some time with a new employee.

Another important reason to spend time with employees is to glean an understanding of the actual operation and assess staff morale. This time is not meant to promote your micromanagement tendencies, but to actually get to know the employees and the work they do.

As I walked around in the training venues to observe training and chat with staff, not only did the employees and students appreciate my engagement, it was rewarding for me to see the instructors thrive in their environment.

The worst leaders are so hierarchical that they don't take time to get to know all levels of employees. These types of leaders might experience some short-term success but will eventually increase bureaucracy and cause morale issues.

Talk to everyone from time to time. It doesn't have to be formal or a big deal. Just make sure you're walking around, chatting, listening. When staff see that you're interested in them and not just in their performance, you will establish trust, strong bonds, and will surely strengthen morale. Many of the best ideas for your organization will come from places you wouldn't expect, so make sure to regularly walk around, observe, and converse.

DL #70: Climb off your high horse and mingle with your team. How long has it been since you met with line staff? There's no time like the present.

CHAPTER 15: CLEAR VISION

This next one might sound odd.

Look, any veteran manager will have some bizarre stories. This is the value of informal coffee talk—you get to hear about all the crazy things that happen, but which don't often make it into management literature.

One day I was meeting with a staff member who was not the model employee. While he was talented, he was paranoid. I was told he kept a journal on all of the managers that he "could use against them if needed." I promise I'm not making this up. If you're new to management, these types of things are uncommon, but they happen!

At one point, this employee made a derogatory statement about another instructor in the presence of students. Hence the meeting. After addressing the alleged conduct, which he downplayed as just joking around, he blurted out to me that he was confused as to the direction of the Academy. While I think there was an ulterior motive, he asked me where the Academy was heading.

At that point, I quoted the vision statement. Then he replied, "What's that really mean?"

I was stunned and taken aback. I did my best to come up with an intelligent answer, but he knew he had me in a corner. I'd brought him in to address his conduct, and yet I ended up on the defensive. How did that happen? Why was I at a loss for words?

After that encounter, I placed more focus on developing very clear statements of vision and mission.

Think about it. Can you and your employees pass the elevator test? That is to say, can you give a clear vision of your organization, its mission, and its brand, while riding with someone on a short elevator ride? Apparently, I needed to go from the ground level to the eighty-seventh floor!

As I began to research the importance of vision, mission, and brand, one thing became crystal clear—many employees do not have an intrinsic connection with these important components.

To be successful, all managers, staff, and internal and external stakeholders must know where they're headed, how to get there, why this is the best destination, the desired image of the organization as a whole and of their team specifically, and the value of the journey.

In essence, vision, mission, and brand are vital to an organization's success, and improving the motivation and buy-in from staff and stake holders.

VISION STATEMENT

The vision statement is a look into the future. It reveals where the organization wants to go.

For example, Starbucks®' vision statement is: To establish Starbucks® as the premier purveyor of the finest coffee in the world while maintaining our uncompromising principles while we grow.

MISSION STATEMENT

The mission statement reveals how to get there—the process. The mission statement is very specific to the values and purpose of each agency.

Starbucks®' mission statement is: To inspire and nurture the human spirit—one person, one cup, and one neighborhood at a time.

VALUES

Values represent the ideas the business believes are most important and are reflected in their standards.

Starbucks®' values are: Creating a culture of warmth and belonging where everyone is welcome. Acting with courage, challenging the status quo and finding new ways to grow our company and each other. Being present, connecting with transparency, dignity, and respect. Delivering our very best in all we do, holding ourselves accountable for results. We are performance-driven, through the lens of humanity.

BRAND

The brand is the personality or image the organization wishes to convey. This may include names, logos, slogans, copy, and other messaging strategies.

Starbucks®' Brand is: To be a company that brings more to the world than a great cup of coffee.

In most instances, the vision statement and brand are more permanent. The vision statement is the overarching goal of the company, and the brand is its personality.

Conversely, the mission statement can be more fluid.

For example, regulations or laws may change, the company may need a change in strategy based on sales, environmental requirements, or other factors, and there may be breakthroughs in technology or a pandemic, etc.

To be successful, it is vital to dissect your organization's vision, mission, and brand. This should include an understanding of the company's values, employee functions, processes, marketing strategies, competitors, economic trends, and environmental factors. These statements should be integrated throughout the organization and should be promoted by all managers, which will inspire staff at all levels.

Even if senior executives aren't communicating it to you when you join up, you should nevertheless study and get a deep understanding of these elements. If you're leading a small or unique team within the organization, or if you're a small business or startup, you might need to develop these yourself or in collaboration with others, if they don't already exist.

INTEGRATION

You've got to realize that vision and mission aren't just about giving a motivational speech or adding these statements to your organization's website. That's insufficient.

In addition to line staff and middle managers understanding the overall vision, it is vital to get all staff and managers regularly to promote the vision and its importance.

Often, employees don't believe in the work they're doing. Thus, the vision and mission statements are hollow documents and the brand is inconsequential. By emphasizing the importance of the work and how it is germane to each employee, you will get much more commitment from staff.

Remember, the vision and mission statements and brand integrity should always be the basis for making major decisions related to the company.

For example, if a company makes brake pads and the vision is to make the most durable and safest brake pads in the world, managers shouldn't make decisions that are contrary to their vision. With this in mind, if a middle manager advises his superiors that he has found a Kevlar-like substance that is cheaper than actual Kevlar and will save the company thousands and thousands of dollars, the leaders should fall back to the vision and mission statements and determine if the cheaper substance will undermine their values. If the substance is not as durable as actual Kevlar, the cheaper substance should be denied.

And again, this isn't just about the managers. You know you're succeeding when staff know the vision and mission by heart, believe in it, and do their work and encourage each other to live it.

DL #71: Managers must make sure that staff at all levels know the company's vision, mission, and brand. They should also help solidify a nexus to their importance.

CHAPTER 16: CREATE A POSITIVE CULTURE

What is culture?

Culture refers to the beliefs and behaviors that determine how team members and management interact with each other and with stakeholders. In a great culture, employees are highly satisfied and feel safe, respected, and valued.

While you'll still have to police bad behavior from time to time, a great culture removes a majority of behavioral problems.

And it starts at the top.

When James Duff returned to the Administrative Office (AO) of the U.S. Courts, on January 5, 2015, as the director, he declared, "The AO endeavors to be the best service organization and the best place to work in the federal government."

Think about that. The federal government is very large. And Director Duff came out and said he's aiming for nothing less than being the best place to work.

Would you want to work for someone like that? Yes! And I really did enjoy working for him tremendously.

Take it apart a little and you'll see three components in Director Duff's statement that are vital to creating a culture of motivation:

- Service: When employees understand the intrinsic value of serving others, it acts as a natural motivation factor;

- Best place to work: Managers must have the goal to promote a culture where employees are pleased with their work environment, colleagues and managers;
- Best agency: There should be a comparison to other agencies and businesses. This sets the tone to become the best in the business.

Make no mistake, this will take time.

Now, this didn't just go on a website or into a single speech. Director Duff repeated this sentiment in nearly every meeting, inspiring managers to find ways to make this goal become the culture of the AO. I could feel the motivation in that statement, and I, along with other managers, began to process ways to adopt this philosophy and inspire our staff to adopt it as well.

When senior management and midlevel managers combine forces to improve culture, they can overcome nearly any obstacle. With that goal in place, everyone should be included to make it a reality. Consider assembling a team made up of all levels of staff with a goal toward improving the culture. Be open to feedback and watch the magic.

DL #72: Culture begins at the top and trickles down.

PART IV

NINJA TRAINING

Time to kick your butt.

Just kidding. Or, half-kidding. I've done some things that are a lot like ninja training, both martial arts and law enforcement.

But even if you're never preparing for a brawl, taking training seriously pays huge dividends. Unfortunately, most organizations aren't really on the cutting edge of training.

Take note, I'm going to go deep on dynamic training. This might be beyond your current role and duties, so feel free to skip this part if that's the case. But, I highly recommend you take the dive with me.

I want to go deep on training because of how powerful it is.

CHAPTER 17: A TRAINING MINDSET

Okay, first, I'd like to share something about my approach to life.

The reason I call this Ninja Training is that I believe we should approach training, and life itself, like we're the guardians of the temple, ready to do battle. We should seek as much training as possible and couple that with life experiences to become like ninjas.

So many people never come close to reaching their potential. When I started training in the martial arts, I pushed my mind and body to limits I had never gone to before. I progressed in ways I hadn't thought possible.

When it comes to training, it is often viewed as something you simply check off your list. Some of this is because of lackluster training programs and presenters, but some of it is about attitude.

There are some specific knowledge, skills, and research you need to know about how to put together really incredible immersive training. I encourage you to start developing exceptional training within your organization. It's very powerful.

So, let's kick it up a notch—pun intended—and take a fresh look at training. Get ready to reap some serious benefits!

LACK OF TRAINING

While you might be in a field that doesn't feel as high stakes as law enforcement, I know from experience that the principles of great training transfer incredibly well to all type of skills and work performance.

But we don't get things perfect all the time either.

A story as example. As mentioned earlier, before we had a national training academy, officers participated in a two-week orientation that was primarily geared toward fundamentals, such as report writing, testifying skills, etc. But it didn't include realistic training to develop skills in areas like conducting proper home visits to offenders under supervision.

Once I was conducting a home visit on a person who was considered dangerous. I had another U.S. probation officer with me, who primarily wrote reports for the court. He was transitioning to the supervision unit. He had some experience, but as you will see, he lacked training.

I briefed him on the details of this individual and noted that, while we always adhered to safety protocol, this guy had a history of conflict with law enforcement. Therefore, we needed to be extra vigilant.

When we entered the residence, the other officer literally sat down and started watching a TV program while I walked with the offender to inspect the house.

I was so furious that I could barely concentrate. When the visit was finally over, I couldn't wait to get back to the car to have a not-so-friendly discussion. When I asked him why he sat down and watched TV, he stated he wanted the person under supervision to feel comfortable.

I agreed it is important to make people feel comfortable, but I asked, "What if something had gone wrong when I was upstairs?" He replied, "I would have run up and helped you."

I asked, "How would you even know what room I was in?" He replied, "The house wasn't that big, I'm sure I could find you."

I then asked how he knew for sure that another person wasn't in the house. He said, "You asked the offender and he said no one else was there."

I was quite frustrated and asked, "Do you think he could have lied?" The officer acknowledged that was a possibility.

I went on to explain that his actions did not promote officer safety. I told him that while the primary officer is addressing the person under supervision, the secondary officer should be alert to the surroundings and that they should never lose contact with each other.

Then, he said the magic words, "I've never been trained on home visits." I wanted to say, "You think!?"

You'd be surprised at how common this is, even in critical situations. We've since rectified that gap in training. But the thing is, you can't expect people to perform well at things they haven't learned.

Even in situations that are less high stakes, good training will save you so much time and aggravation.

ZZZZZZZZ

Some people become complacent and lose their desire to learn new information or to broaden their interactions. If you fall into this category, it's time to get out of the rut. Training is vital, particularly with new responsibilities, software programs, equipment, etc.

I understand. If we're honest here, and I asked you to list three takeaways from a recent training program and how you implemented those lessons into your day-to-day responsibilities, could you provide an answer?

For most people, it's no.

Part of the problem is often the presenter.

I was in a training program recently, and the presenter was so monotone and boring that I thought to myself, she should teach a master class on sleep enhancement. She was not a ninja!

Before we delve into effective learning, let's take a look at some dos and don'ts for instructors.

EFFECTIVE PRESENTERS

When I was in sixth grade, we had a teacher by the name of Bill Parish. Not only was he an effective communicator, he knew the power of a good story. During our free time, he read Black Beauty and Robin Hood to us over the course of the year. I remember looking forward to reading time. He would read some parts of the book and then allow time for discussion. He made the stories come alive, and we respected him as a teacher.

A quality presenter usually starts with a "hook."

This is usually an interesting and relatable story that gets the participants' attention. Stories are very effective and can enhance learning and retention.

If you're instructing or presenting, it's critical to have knowledge and convey passion about the topic. The same applies if you're looking to bring in an outside trainer and are deciding who to select. In those cases, look to find a video file of them instructing and see if they're really knowledgeable and show a passion for their work.

As for yourself, these are skills. You practice them and get better. While conducting training especially, you must learn to read a participant's body language and level of involvement. This might sound obvious, but you've got to avoid monotone statements and find ways to engage the group.

I used to teach an instructor development program, and I would begin the class by setting up two blank charts.

Then I would ask the participants to describe in a sentence or a word one of their best and worst professors, instructors, or teachers. We started with the worst, which seemed to be somewhat therapeutic for the officers. In every class the chart would be full.

In the worst category, there would be statements or words such as boring, lacking subject matter knowledge, uninterested, distracting habits, failure to engage students. The positive category included such things as engaging, knowledgeable, passionate, motivating, and demonstrative.

Whether you are charged with selecting a presenter for your team, or you have to make a presentation yourself, the points above are important to remember.

Think back to an effective training program you attended. It probably consisted of a good presenter and impactful content. Both are equally important. And both can be learned.

DEVELOPING IMPACTFUL CONTENT

While you may not have someone formally trained in instructional design, you can still develop effective training programs. In addition to conferring with subject matter experts, it is vital to develop training that is relatable to all learning styles.

LEARNING STYLES

Visual: Learn more effectively when they see information such as slides, graphs, charts, etc.

Auditory: Learn better when hearing information, such as lectures and discussion.

Tactile or kinesthetic: Learn more through physical activities, such as breakout exercises and practical exercises.

Unfortunately, most training programs are geared toward visual and auditory learners, and tend to provide little, if any, real learning opportunities for kinesthetic participants.

This explains why I, along with many other people attending leadership training programs, only retained minimal information.

PERFORMANCE BASED EXERCISES
FOR DYNAMIC TRAINING

All right, let's get into one of the coolest concepts I can teach you. This single thing, by itself, might just be enough to put your training presentations at the top ten percent of what attendees ever experience.

A dynamic training program will cater to all types of learners.

While breakout groups are the most popular method used to keep participants involved, I've found a more dynamic approach that is not included in most training programs.

Performance-based role play.

One example of this is where participants are placed in high stress environments, such as providing an employee with constructive feedback, and taught to overcome the physiological stress often experienced in these encounters.

There are two general ways to minimize anxiety during stressful situations, which results in what is known as physiological resilience.

Grounded Breathing: Participants should take a deep breath just before beginning the exercise. This one breath disrupts increased heart rate and heavy breathing and helps stabilize blood and oxygen flow. This breathing exercise, coupled with repetitive practice of these types of scenarios, can help create physiological resilience.

Many law enforcement agencies teach grounded breathing techniques to help officers focus during life and death encounters. The stress experienced in these situations is often called fight or flight—being the physiological factors of fear.

When I was introduced to the concept of taking one deep, grounded breath before and after stressful scenarios, I quickly realized this was a game changer.

Repetition: Participants should be asked to repeat the practical exercises, to allow for improvement and minimize stress. Repeating an exercise also increases the level of comfort and builds confidence.

Once, I attended a tactical training course which culminated in a simulated lethal force situation. Part of the exercise required participants to perform physically strenuous activities and then unlock a door with a key before engaging an assailant with non-lethal force weapons like paintballs. Toward the end of the exercise, after I had sprinted, climbed a wall, crawled through a drainpipe, and defended myself from a mock physical attack, I experienced an adrenaline dump. I was breathing heavily and became lightheaded as the blood rushed to my brain.

It was very difficult to get the key into the lock, as my fine motor skills were compromised. Next, the assailant role player began shooting the non-lethal rounds at me. When I returned fire, I missed several times before hitting the mark.

You have probably experienced these physiological responses if you have ever been in an automobile accident, suffered from a fall, or maybe when you had to confront someone in an intense situation.

Other reactions to these encounters can cause tunnel vision, where we lose sight of our peripheral surroundings, or it can cause us to perceive that everything is happening in slow motion—as I experienced when I witnessed the shooting at the Police Academy. After the incident, we may feel weak and exhausted. This is due to our nervous system's response.

The fact is, people can fail to perform because they don't know what to do at all, due to a lack of training, policies, or guidance. Or people do know these things, but still aren't able to perform in high-stress situations such as closing an important sale, a confrontation, or giving difficult feedback. Often, people don't realize they can condition themselves to be better under pressure and thereby experience less anxiety.

That's what performance-based exercises are geared to do. They mimic real life.

AUTONOMIC NERVOUS SYSTEM, BRIEFLY

I'm not going to try to give you a full science textbook explanation, but I'd like to encourage you to study up a little on how the human nervous system works.

Obviously, it has life-or-death consequences for law enforcement officers, so we take this topic quite seriously.

But it's that very same fight or flight response that comes if a customer is angry and shouting, or if unexpected bad news hits. It's the same biology behind the response.

Briefly, the parasympathetic nervous system keeps us calm, but in a dangerous encounter, the sympathetic nervous system takes over to prepare us for perceived danger. That is the fight or flight response. When you begin to calm down, the parasympathetic nervous system starts to regain control, leaving you with a feeling of exhaustion and dizziness.

I encourage you to study up on this as your management responsibilities grow. The ability to handle stress well and to help your team deal with it is a key part of excellent performance and wellbeing.

The nice thing is, when you put together realistic performance-based training, it helps people experience the actual rush of the sympathetic nervous system taking over, followed by the crash when returning to parasympathetic. They get used to it, adapt to it, and perform better. Safely simulating stressful situations in practice can help you and your team overcome these normal physiological responses in real world scenarios.

That being said, good training exercises alone aren't enough. It's also essential to debrief effectively.

EFFECTIVE DEBRIEFS

Without a debriefing process, it is difficult to gauge how well your team is learning and retaining information and neglects a great opportunity for immediate growth.

When you debrief with team members after a training exercise, each trainee should share their perception of their own performance as well as their perception of other participants. Then the instructor should provide similar feedback.

The debrief should include the following: 1) What went well for each participant, 2) What could be improved upon and 3) Their anxiety level on a scale of one to five.

What went well: This allows participants to focus in on their own strengths during the scenario or dynamic exercise. The other students and an instructor should provide them with positive feedback as well. Usually, all participants do some things well, which is important to discuss.

What could they improve upon: In most cases, students tend to be their own worst critic; therefore, it is important keep the negativity at a minimum but to provide a proper assessment. Remember, psychological training scars can occur if the process is too negative.

Anxiety level rating: This is vital and is designed for the participant to discuss their intrinsic stress level during the exercise, such as increased heart rate, dizziness, increased breathing, etc.

A quick note: In a low-trust corporate culture, this is hard to do. That's where the expectations document, vision, and mission come in. When the team is excited to learn and grow and work together, the debrief is an exciting process, which is highly engaging and enjoyable.

PRACTICAL APPLICATION IN MANAGEMENT

I was inspired to develop 4Ward Management Coaching when I realized that the majority of management and leadership training programs that I'd attended had been only lectures with PowerPoint presentations and lacked the type of gritty performance-based exercises I was accustomed to from law enforcement.

I began to approach key difficult management decisions and actions with the same lens and thoroughness of federal law enforcement training. And I began to rehearse and role-play management conflicts and decisions much the same way I'd learned, developed curriculum, and trained to prepare for dangerous situations in the law enforcement world.

Later, I prepared scripts to rehearse, added the process of speaking positive outcomes, visualizing successful meetings, practicing grounded breathing exercises, and role-playing situations.

You know, at first people might have thought I was crazy. We were practicing and preparing for management and office skills with the same seriousness we'd approach tactical exercises on the firing range. But as I completed this process on a regular basis, the outcomes were astounding.

Before some of the managers I was training from various agencies had to make challenging phone calls, meet with employees to discuss personnel actions, or made difficult decisions, I practiced these techniques with them. We learned to ground ourselves quickly with deep breaths before proceeding. We learned to keep our stress levels in check.

Performance went up a lot. And happiness. And morale. And…everything is good.

Now a few more tools for you to use to help your team develop.

DYNAMIC ROLE PLAY

Role Playing difficult situations is a very powerful tool that can help your team prepare and perform when something difficult is coming up, as well as being a way to build a general foundation of skills and resiliency for when unexpected difficult situations arise. The process will work in your personal life as well. You *can* master confrontation. Start small and build your confidence.

Some years ago, Lisa, a manager, told me that she had to confront a tenured employee named Matt. Matt had been with the agency much longer than Lisa, but his performance had started deteriorating. Lisa confided that this looming encounter was causing her a lot of anxiety. So, I told her about my new scripting and scenario-based approach to these encounters and offered to walk her through the process.

She accepted.

I helped Lisa develop a script with the basic information she wanted to convey to Matt, which included a grounding breath, an introduction, an overview, the importance of empathetic listening—listening to understand and empathize, if needed—visualization, consequences, and a conclusion.

As we role-played the situation, we began to brainstorm things that Matt might say to derail the meeting. Each time we acted out the scenario, Lisa improved her delivery and responses. She began visualizing a successful outcome, and I could literally see her confidence build as we continued to practice.

A couple of days later, Lisa contacted me and said the meeting with Matt went very well. She said the role-play came back to her, and she clearly and concisely conveyed all of the information from the script. When she started to grovel a little toward the end of the meeting, she remembered that was a mistake, and corrected it immediately. The encounter was a big success.

She told me that another manager had informed her that Matt had shared the details of their meeting and that other employees seemed pleased someone had finally addressed Matt's poor performance. Bam!

I've realized that most managers already have the ability to form a good script. They just need practice in order to build the courage to deliver it.

DL #73: Practice strategies and techniques to minimize fear through repetition.

TRAINING EVALUATIONS

There are a couple of obvious barriers to training. Many people don't see the value in it, no doubt because they've never been part of really great training.

Once you realize the importance of it, there are skills to learn and practice. Training benefits from learning about human physiology and how people learn, and then putting in the time to customize realistic scenarios that are relevant to the skills your team needs to perform.

However, I'd be remiss if I didn't say that, once your training starts going well, it's easy to become complacent. The biggest reason many training programs do not improve is because they do not solicit objective ways to evaluate the effectiveness of the training.

Usually, a trainer distributes an evaluation sheet at the end of the program that asks some simple questions with a scale of one to five, with five being the highest score. Then there is a section for additional comments. If that is the only evaluation method, consider the following:

1) These evaluations are administered at the end of the program when participants are usually tired and ready to leave.

2) Participants may simply have enjoyed the delivery method of the training and instructor, which may cloud their judgment as to the merits of the material.

3) Participants haven't had to time to digest the information.

4) Participants have not had an opportunity to determine if the information is transferable to their actual duties and responsibilities.

5) There is no method of long-term follow-up to determine if the training had any impact after a few months on the job.

6) Evaluator concerns. While opinions vary on this topic, just be cognizant that some participants might be hesitant to include their true objective feedback.

Here's an awkward moment when I was an instructor that validates my point on the ineffectiveness of after-class evaluations.

When the academy first opened in 2005, I was asked to teach a class on Financial Investigations. I helped establish a team to develop a lesson plan and a presentation. I led the team with the assistance of a U.S. probation officer who held a PhD and was considered a financial investigations expert. She also agreed to teach the first few iterations of the class, while I and another instructor would observe, then would eventually take over the teaching responsibilities.

During the second iteration of the class, I was sitting in the back of the classroom with the class materials to observe one more time before teaching the class. About ten minutes before the class began, I learned there had been a scheduling error, so I was going to have to teach this class.

I remember the awkward feeling of walking to the front of the class, accessing the PowerPoint presentation, turning around to face the student officers, and saying with as much confidence as I could muster, "Welcome to Financial Investigations."

I taught the class but struggled with some of the content. The students asked a couple of questions that I couldn't answer, but I survived. My presentation ability was strong, but the content coverage of the material was mediocre at best.

Up to this point, I had always gotten excellent scores on the after-class evaluations. So much for my great record.

When these evaluations were available the following Monday, I was apprehensive but took a breath and began to search for that particular class. To my utter surprise, I had gotten a five in all categories. Five was the highest possible score.

Why?

At that moment, I came to realize the subjective nature of the class evaluations. I surmised the probable reason was the fact that I had already developed rapport with the students during defensive tactics and other classes where I was more proficient. So, basically, they already liked me.

This experience validates my point that written evaluations do not always equate to quality training.

The following is the process used by accredited federal law enforcement programs:

1) Initial Response: The traditional method of end-of-class feedback can be used to glean an initial response from participants, but don't forget the disclaimers noted previously.

2) Learning: Did the participant's knowledge and skills improve? This is determined through various assessments, such as written or online testing, practical exercises, etc.

3) Implementation: Did the participant later implement any of the principles or skills gleaned from the training program? This can be done by having the participant and participant's supervisor complete an assessment six to twelve months after the training program. This gauges job readiness and overall success.

4) Results: What was the effect of the training on the business as a whole? For example, have sales increased?

At the Academy, we applied the first three of the four methods of the evaluation process.

If you have the time and resources to follow up after the training, here is some information to consider.

A SUGGESTED FOLLOW-UP FORM

Follow Up on (Name of Course) (date(s) of training) (location of training)

1) What were the strengths and weaknesses of the instructor's delivery? Explain.

2) What were the strengths and weaknesses of the course content? Explain.

3) Has your opinion of the training changed since returning to work? Explain.

4) Have you implemented any of the information into your daily responsibilities? Explain.

5) Has the training changed your perspective on any particular job function? Explain.

6) Would you change any component of the training? Explain.

7) Would you recommend this training to your colleagues in the future? Explain.

This is an extensive process that may not be possible in some situations. However, this comprehensive evaluation method is sure to improve training programs.

At minimum, in addition to the after-class evaluation sheet, managers should follow up with staff a few weeks or months after the training to obtain a post-training perspective. This can be done via another written evaluation with a scoring system, but an explanation should be asked for with each answer. Once again, if this is not feasible for your organization, at least have a follow-up personal conversation with staff. The feedback you'll get is priceless.

Just be sure to remember, if they liked the trainer personally, they'll give them good marks. So, don't forget to look out for actual improvement over time.

PART V

CONSTRUCTIVE FEEDBACK
AND CONFRONTATION

I hope I've got the gears turning in your mind about training. In particular, about the importance of creating realistic role-playing scenarios.

Now we are going to talk about what many managers believe is the most difficult part of leadership: Confrontation and addressing negative behaviors.

If you've established yourself well and put in a strong management foundation, these behaviors should be less frequent.

Even if you've got clear expectations and a great culture, problems do arise and you're going to have to deal with them. And you're going to need courage to do so.

CHAPTER 18: FEAR

It might not be an exaggeration to say part of becoming a great leader is like being on a quest to minimize fear.

Not only will addressing your fears help you manage better at work, there may be situations when you must confront a family member, a friend, or even a stranger. It's just a reality of life.

I have been honest about my early struggles with workplace confrontation, particularly when it involved a personnel action.

Don't get me wrong, I certainly had the courage to confront people in other situations, including a rough-looking biker dude who blocked my car in and said that I had cut in front of him on the highway. Boy did he get a surprise! In short, I had some words for him and gave him three seconds to move his bike. Thank God, he rode away.

If you struggle with straight-forward conversations or with any form of confrontation, don't beat yourself up. Remember, fear is compartmentalized. We all have courage, and we all have fears. But trust me when I tell you that most any fear can be minimized by practicing.

It's totally understandable that many people fear confrontation. Even the general dictionary definition of confrontation uses words like "hostile" or "argumentative." When you have to confront someone, there seems to be a thousand things that can go wrong. It's easy to worry that you could get too nervous, say something stupid, cave under pressure, be too soft in the delivery, request an impossible outcome, and the list goes on and on.

You must get beyond that type of thinking.

I had arrested people and competed in karate tournaments before going into management, but the act of confronting someone's behavior and taking personnel action...well, it produced a new type of anxiety for me.

After I did a deep dive into my insecurity along with a lot of intro-spection, I figured out my problem. It was rooted in my background. We've discussed my limited exposure to culture, education, and com-mercialism in my formative years. And I had to confront employees who had more diverse backgrounds than mine, who went to better universities, grew up in the big city, and probably went to McDonald's for a burger before the age of nine.

To counter this, I read leadership books and articles on how to deal with difficult people, I watched videos on the subject, and I participat-ed in several leadership training programs.

That should do the trick, right?

Nope.

I still got extremely nervous when confronting behavior in the workplace. After stammering my way through the situation described in the preface of this book, I quickly realized that to be successful, I had to overcome this insecurity. I knew that I wasn't a coward, but I still had this nagging fear.

Then it hit me. I remembered that I once worked with a guy who would fight a circular saw, but if he saw a spider, he would panic and scream like a baby pig calling for its mother.

I repeat: Fear is compartmentalized. We can be brave in one area and fearful in another.

You improve both through practice and through developing strat-egies for situations you're going to face. While there are ten million possible scenarios that could come up, I want to help you get prepared for a mix of some of the most common, and a few that are likely to catch you by surprise.

DL #74: Good managers don't allow staff pedigree, education, or background to intimidate them. Instead, they embrace the authority vested in them and take the necessary steps to build confidence.

CHAPTER 19: CONSTRUCTIVE PERFORMANCE REVIEWS

Performance reviews will be among the most unpleasant things you have to do with some regularity. In my many conversations with managers, this is one of their least favorite activities. So, you're not alone.

The evaluation process has been debated for years, and multiple instruments and methodologies are used throughout different companies and agencies. Regardless of the instrument, you as the manager are the key to a successful performance plan and evaluation process.

Other problems often arise when you're focusing hard on providing objective feedback to the exclusion of everything else. Even if you have been working on your assertiveness, you still have to provide feedback with empathy, honesty, and finesse.

I worked for a manager we'll call Jason. Jason had no problem with confrontation. As a matter of fact, I think he liked it.

However, there was one major problem. He was great at pointing out problems but offered no real solutions. Not to mention, his delivery was terrible.

Once Jason assigned me to be the training officer for a new employee, we'll call Bill.

Bill wasn't a great writer, and he had made several mistakes on a report. As Bill and I were working through some of the issues, Jason walked into my office and asked what we were doing.

I didn't say anything, but Bill began to show him the report.

Jason barked, "This report will ultimately go to a judge, so you better get it right." Then he got up and walked out. Thanks for the tip, Jason. Bill was visibly nervous. I assured him that he would improve if he kept working hard.

Managers owe it to themselves and their employees to conduct fair and objective evaluations, offer viable solutions, and provide steps to improve. A good manager knows his or her employees, is keenly aware of their responsibilities, and provides regular feedback to promote success.

When feedback is a regular occurrence, there should be no surprises when it is time for the annual performance review.

During regular meetings between managers and employees, there are eight words that can change the dynamic of the entire organization.

Ready? Here they are.

Are you getting what you need from me?

Imagine a world where managers ask their employees those eight words and an honest dialogue ensues. If you'll ask that regularly, and you've built a high-trust culture, you'll be amazed at the valuable information you'll get.

Now, let's consider a world where the employee asks her supervisor the same eight words. Are you getting what you need from me? And, more honest and open discussion takes place.

This might be uncomfortable at first. But eventually, it will become part of the fabric of the organization. Then sit back and watch the magic!

Seriously, if there's one single thing you take from this book and implement, make it those eight words:

Are you getting what you need from me?

Try it out. Include it regularly as part of evaluations and feedback.

One other consideration when providing constructive feedback is to get as many facts as possible in order to ensure you haven't been misinformed and that you are unbiased. At the meeting, it is vital to listen carefully and weigh all aspects of an issue to make an objective assessment.

Performance evaluations can be awesome coaching opportunities if done correctly.

When I taught defensive tactics, at the end of each class other instructors and I would debrief the day's training and instructor performance together in a peer review. This was difficult at first, but once it became part of the culture, our instructors' performances improved exponentially. In fact, they rarely made the same mistake twice.

Honest Feedback + Understanding + Practice = Improvement.

DL #75: Performance reviews should be an extension of ongoing, honest, and open dialogue between managers and employees, and should rarely produce any surprises.

FAILURE TO IMPROVE

The dirty truth is there will be times when your coaching and feedback does not produce the intended results and you'll have to take the unhappy but necessary steps to correct the situation.

Once again, this takes courage and finesse.

When conduct must be addressed in a performance evaluation, I have developed the Ward Method of feedback, outlined in the table below to assist.

Remember to form your script and practice before the meeting. With a slight variation, this method can be used in nearly all meetings where constructive feedback is needed.

THE WARD METHOD OF FEEDBACK FOR NEGATIVE PERFORMANCE

Schedule meeting	Meeting	After meeting
• Schedule in writing at least 24 hours in advance • Be clear on the purpose of the meeting • Predetermine the meeting location (Consider using the employee's office to promote a more comfortable environment)	• Give a pleasant greeting, but keep small talk at a minimum (will seem disingenuous) • Summarize previous meetings and attempts at improvement • Be clear that the desired level of improvement has not been attained (Always consider the employee's personal wellbeing but outside of rare circumstances, continue the feedback) • Discuss each area in the evaluation and be clear as to why an area was not satisfactory • Ask the employee for an explanation (don't accept the same excuses). • Include the employee in developing an improvement plan • Advise the employee that regular meetings will be scheduled to gauge improvement, and schedule the next meeting (give about two weeks unless an immediate meeting is needed) • End the meeting with optimism, but be clear that improvement is expected within a certain timeframe	• Make an informal follow up within 48 hours to keep communication flowing and to convey that the process isn't personal. Then have a formal follow up in two weeks

As a side note, in-person feedback may not be possible during the Covid-19 pandemic or for employees who work remotely. In those instances, rather than just a phone call, try to use video conferencing or another platform to allow a more personal conversation. Body language and eye contact are vital during these encounters.

If a meeting becomes unproductive, or if the employee becomes too emotional, end the meeting and reschedule within a few days.

By having a method in place, you will perform much more succinctly and avoid the pitfall of saying something that could derail the meeting or be used against you later. You are also more likely to see subsequent employee improvement, which is after all the goal, right?

Remember, this is a dirty side of leadership that cannot be avoided. However, if you adopt an effective feedback method, you are more likely to gain an edge and experience success for yourself and your employees.

DL #76: A proper feedback method will keep the meeting on track and expedite employee improvement.

CHAPTER 20: WE'VE GOT YOUR SIX

For you non-law enforcement readers, when your partner says, "I've got your six," she is saying, "I've got your back." It's based on the numbers on a clock. Get it?

Ever think you could get your whole company involved in a conflict? It's possible. It happened to me once.

Conflict is not always between two individuals but can also arise between two companies.

Company vs. company conflicts, lawsuits, and the like are almost routine in business. It could involve a competitor spreading rumors about another company, or even intellectual property theft.

Whether this ever happens to you or not, one thing is vital. You must be confident that your organization will support you. I have a unique story to corroborate my point.

Several years ago, I had to write a pre-sentence report on a female inmate who had escaped from a minimum-security federal complex. As I interviewed her, I suspected she had assistance getting out of town once she had left the facility. At first, she said she hitched a ride with a long-haul trucker at a truck stop.

When I asked how she got to the truck stop, she said, "I think I caught a ride with a guy in a pickup truck." She clearly wasn't telling the truth; she was simply too vague.

At that point, to persuade her to tell the truth I used the sentencing guideline provision of acceptance of responsibility, which states that if someone is truthful, they can get a reduction in their sentencing guideline calculation, which can lead to a sentence reduction. At that point she told me she had acquired a pen pal who'd developed affection for her, and he'd met her outside of the prison gate.

After the interview, I went to the jail administrators and got the names on her visitor list. Sure enough, her new love interest was on the list. I got his name and social security number and called the U.S. Attorney's office.

I left feeling like a hero.

But the following morning, Dr. Samples, my chief, called me to let me know the U.S. Marshal Service had sent him a letter of complaint against me.

I was stunned! I thought I had done some great investigative work.

They asserted I had taken over their investigation.

After I explained my actions to Dr. Samples, he assured me I had operated within protocol and complimented me on my work.

However, he called back later to let me know the U.S. Marshal and his deputy were driving to my office the following day for a meeting.

Dr. Samples assured me that he and his deputy would be there as well. He had my six.

Since I was relatively new to the position, the prospect of the meeting was a little unnerving.

I was honestly a little worried. I felt I'd done great work, well within the scope of my duties, and the whole complaint was really surprising and bizarre to me.

So, everyone arrived. We gathered in a small room and placed some chairs in a circle. And then—I'll never forget this—Dr. Samples explained my actions and asserted I had operated within protocol and advised everyone he was shredding the letter of complaint.

The U.S. Marshal had no rebuttal except that I should have called their office instead of the U.S. Attorney. The only problem was, I wasn't under any obligation to call them. Frankly, I think the guys on that case were a little embarrassed that no one had followed up on the jail visitor list.

I should note, the U.S. Marshal service is outstanding, and I worked closely with them as a U.S. probation officer. This incident was an anomaly.

Strange anomalies do happen, and that's where knowing you've got support from the top is key. You always cultivate a great relationship with your superiors from day one, and if and when something like this happens to you, communicate clearly and see if you'll be supported.

Dr. Samples supported me, and the courage he exhibited had a profound impact on me and certainly taught me to stand up for what is right.

DL #77: A reputable company must support employee actions as long as they are legal and within policy.

CHAPTER 21: GENERATIONAL CONFLICT

UNDERSTANDING GENERATIONAL DIFFERENCES

Over the past fifteen to twenty years, there has been a trend occurring in most businesses. Senior citizens have become very active in the workplace. I read a statistic that twenty percent of people sixty-five and older are still working.

In other words, it is not uncommon for a twenty-two-year-old and a seventy year-old to be working side by side. This can be a wonderful dynamic but can also create issues that you will have to address.

Many managers I have talked with have mixed feelings about different age groups.

They believe Baby Boomers—born between 1944-1965—and Gen X workers—born between 1965-1979—are more loyal and dedicated and have strong interpersonal skills. Yet, many of the older employees lack the technology skills that are often needed.

They also expressed mixed opinions on the up-and-coming generations.

Managers noted Gen Y and Millennials—born 1980-1994—have certain traits in common. Most have great technological skills, they're good problem-solvers, and, due to social media and other sources they're very connected to one another and the world. But they just don't seem to have the same level of loyalty to the company.

To stay on top of age group differences and their respective philosophies, you must keep an open mind and be a transformational leader. To do so, seek relevant training, have conversations, and be respectful and observant of culture, background, and history.

The next story will provide you with some ideas to consider when dealing with generational differences in the workplace.

THE GENERATIONAL DILEMMA

Michelle supervised several employees at a manufacturing company. Among the employees were a twenty-eight-year-old woman named Samantha and a fifty-one-year-old man named Maurice. This relationship resulted in an interesting dynamic.

While both were seemingly nice people, they had trouble working together. One day, Samantha approached Michelle and showed her an app that streamlined production count. Samantha wanted Michelle to approve its purchase. Michelle loved the app and approved the purchase immediately.

Not long after Samantha had the app installed, she asked to meet with Michelle again. During the meeting, Samantha said that Maurice wasn't open to downloading the app on his company phone and didn't believe it would expedite production count.

Michelle decided to talk with Maurice. When questioned, Maurice told her there was no need for the app and that Samantha spent too much time on her cell phone. He believed she was always looking for shortcuts to avoid hard work. He also asserted that she lacked customer service skills.

This presented quite the challenge for Michelle.

Maurice had been with the company for eighteen years. Samantha had already worked for three similar companies but had been with this manufacturer for just ten months. Not only did they approach work differently, they also came from different cultural backgrounds. Samantha had a master's degree, and Maurice was former military with a high school education.

Michelle believed that Samantha had brought several good ideas to the company, but she also admired Maurice's work ethic, his ability to communicate, and his years of service.

As Michelle began to seek middle ground, she tried to get to the root of the problem. While Samantha was more technologically savvy, Michelle observed that Maurice seemed to have better rapport with commercial buyers. Both were hard workers, and Maurice had no problem working overtime. To the contrary, Samantha would try to find a way to complete tasks more efficiently, as she believed overtime was unnecessary. Maurice approached problem-solving in a traditional way. He would analyze the problem, study some literature, and talk with some experts. On the other hand, Samantha would seek the answer online. These are just a few of the differences between the two employees.

Michelle met with Maurice and Samantha and discussed the issues. It seemed to go pretty well. But by the end of the week, the same problems resurfaced.

WORKING OUT GENERATIONAL DIFFERENCES

Michelle called me asking for advice.

The first thing I did was perform a wellness check and give her some much needed encouragement. This is paramount. Next, I explained that a manager cannot change someone's background or historical perspective. However, if employees respect one another, they will find a way to work together.

Michelle asked how she could promote this much-needed respect. I recommended that Maurice and Samantha develop a better understanding of each other's background and perspective. To that end, I suggested that Michelle invite them to lunch and be forthright about the reason—to help them to get to know each other a little better, which might improve their ability to work together and to increase productivity. Employees usually know when you have an ulterior motive, so be clear and honest from the get-go.

Michelle was a bit apprehensive about having such a meeting because she didn't know how she would guide the conversation. I told her to find out beforehand some things that Samantha and Maurice felt comfortable discussing. I suggested that Maurice's military career might be a great topic and that Samantha could talk about her experiences in college. I further explained that it might take more than one lunch to get the two of them aligned.

The next step would be to have Maurice and Samantha work together on a special project, and possibly do some cross-training with each other. Michelle would have to supervise these activities carefully until the two got more comfortable with each other.

A few weeks later, Michelle said that the lunch and subsequent joint project work had been a tremendous success. At lunch, each had stories the other found interesting. They even discussed the differences between baby boomers and millennials and developed some inside jokes to use at work.

IT DOESN'T ALWAYS WORK OUT

Okay. Listen up! The dirty truth is, situations like those I have just addressed don't always have a happy ending. The Maurices and Samanthas of the world may never develop a good working relationship, and if they're on your team, you'll have to establish boundaries and take the appropriate action when necessary to ensure they do their jobs.

To be successful as a manager you must be able to lead people of various ages, backgrounds, ethnicities, sexual orientations, etc. One of the best ways to be effective is to get to know the person. Ask questions. No, it shouldn't include, "How much do you have in your savings account?" or "How well do you get along with your significant other?" But the more you know about your staff, the more effective you will be.

While policy may be etched in stone, you might need to vary the specific details of getting things done, depending on the person.

Another method to address similar situations is to have staff cross-train, in order to share their strengths and talents with one another.

Find ways to relate to all employees. If you're serious about management, take the necessary steps to be relevant in an ever-changing and diverse workplace. If you have been slacking in this area, it's time to backtrack and get to know your staff.

> DL #78: A solid manager realizes that employees have different perspectives and backgrounds but will find ways to leverage each group's gifts and talents and use those strengths to better the agency.

CHAPTER 22: PICK ME!

THE GOAT

Promoting staff is one of the more surprisingly difficult issues that you'll experience.

If you think everyone is going to like you, wait until you have a competitive opening in the office. With nearly all promotions, there is one happy person and several disappointed employees.

There are situations where some of the applicants believe they are the GOAT—the Greatest Of All Time. Some of these people are very talented, and they know it. They believe their talent automatically qualifies them for the promotion. But as any good manager knows, there is more to consider than just talent.

This reminds me of an employee we'll call Chad, who reported to another manager at the Academy. Chad had a reputation for disrespecting his colleagues and was perceived as being arrogant. The manager took steps to verify that Chad, on several occasions, had gossiped about others.

As you might expect, Chad thought he was God's gift to the agency. He even completed a leadership program over a several month period. It is interesting that after all of the leadership principles he studied, his behavior remained the same. Hate to say I warned you about many ineffective leadership training programs, but...

As expected, he applied for a promotion and touted his leadership training in the interview.

Chad was not promoted, and let's just say, I wasn't his favorite person. He absolutely believed he deserved the promotion.

As a matter of fact, he was passed over a few times. Afterward, he spoke to me only when he had to. The sad reality is that Chad would have been a shoo-in for the promotion had his attitude been better and his integrity intact. He eventually left the agency.

A significant number of these types of people are gifted but promoting them would be detrimental to the agency. This would also send the wrong message to the other employees. Just be a talented jerk and you'll get promoted.

Because many people don't have times of introspection and don't come to terms with their own behavior, they're shocked when they learn that they're not the Chosen One.

DL #79: Don't be intimidated or judge solely on talent alone. Instead, select the best candidate for the betterment of the team and hold firm.

THE DECLINATION

Once I had another employee who was passed over for several promotions. On each occasion, I met with him to deliver the message in person. During the last meeting, he simply responded, "I know the drill, don't waste your time." I have to give him credit, he was right.

When giving feedback to internal staff who don't get promoted, you must be careful. Some prior negative conduct or performance issues may not have been documented in an employee's performance evaluations. If you try to bring that conduct into the equation, you might open yourself up to a complaint. Boy, it would sure feel good though.

This is another situation I wasn't prepared to handle early on in my career.

First and foremost, if possible, deliver good news and bad news in person. While it is difficult to inform employees that they didn't get the promotion, at some point they will usually respect you for meeting with them instead of sending an impersonal email.

Some employees will take it in stride and thank you for the opportunity. Others may become angry and want to vent. One thing to remember is to keep these meetings short. When an employee feels deflated, it is not the time to provide feedback.

Once I met with an employee who didn't get promoted. As I began to inform him, he did what we in law enforcement call the thousand-yard stare—when someone gazes over your head and appears emotionally detached from the conversation.

It became obvious that he was upset, so I knew it wasn't the right time to provide feedback. I told him to let me know if he was interested in feedback on his interview or the process and we would schedule a meeting. He never scheduled the meeting, so I guess I made the right call.

At times, employees may need time to vent, so it's best to deliver the news on Friday and let them decompress over the weekend. They do it in politics all the time.

Remember, do not allow yourself to be disrespected. If they start to make accusations or become too emotional, advise them that you're going to give them time to process, and you will be happy to schedule a time to debrief and provide feedback.

The best way to deliver the message is to state that the promotion selection was based on education, responses to interview questions, and overall performance. With this being the focus, you don't have to disparage the employee who was passed over. You can simply explain that the person selected had many great qualities and had won the day.

If the employee asks for a follow-up meeting, schedule it and provide the most objective feedback that you can. Attempt to provide the employee with a plan for improvement, but never lead the person to believe that he or she has the next promotion.

In most cases, the tensions will diminish over time. Don't let this kind of situation affect the big picture. Let the aftermath play out, and in time things will usually go back to normal.

DL #80: In-person meetings, even when delivering bad news, are always the highest form of communication. Don't stress. Usually those who are disappointed will get over it in time.

CHAPTER 23: TATAKAI

LET'S GET IT ON

Except for the rare narcissist, most leaders want their employees to do well and excel in their positions. Yet, it is inevitable that someone will test your fortitude and see what you're made of.

Everyone loves a hero. We love the way they stand up for what's right and oppose evil forces. As Michael Keaton once said in his role as the Batman, "You wanna get nuts? Come on. Let's get nuts!" I'm a huge superhero movie buff.

Unfortunately, there genuinely are some people who take pleasure from seeing other people hurt or humiliated. If you happen to wind up with one of those individuals on a team you inherited, they need to know that somewhere deep in your cortex, buried for special occasions, is a small and measured amount of "you don't want to go there." I know this isn't traditional management literature but talk to an experienced manager and see what they say about it.

I have to say this again because it is so important. Even if you feel intimidated reading this section, I assure you that repetitive practice of the processes outlined in the book will prepare you to meet these difficult challenges. As with any skill-building exercise, it will take some serious practice, but you can do it.

Here is an example of one of the many confrontations I had after I had started building up my level of courage using these same processes.

We had a project that had to be done. So, a few other managers and I solicited employees who had some expertise in the areas needed. We developed a charter—much like a vision statement—for the team, gave some other assignments, and appointed the team leader.

An employee we'll call Dean came to my office and asserted that he didn't think I should have selected that team leader, and he didn't want to work with the person. I explained that the assignments had been made and that I expected Dean to work with the team and contribute to the outcome.

This approach worked for a while, but then Dean was in a group meeting with other managers and colleagues when a group decision was made about a process. Dean vehemently disagreed and forcefully voiced his opposition. Nonetheless, the group voted to stick with its decision. At that point, Dean began to use profanity and stormed out of the room. A few minutes had passed when one of the managers told me what Dean had done. I also spoke with another manager to make sure that I had the facts straight.

At that point, I called Dean on the phone and in no uncertain terms told him that I had been made aware of his behavior and that it would not be tolerated. I demanded that he report to my office first thing the next morning and hung up the phone. This may sound a little over the top, but it was just what ole Dean needed.

Sometimes having an employee wait twenty-four hours can be a good thing. Hopefully, they will have time to cool off while doing some introspection. Sure enough, by the time that Dean came to my office the next day, he was very apologetic. He certainly knew that I was not playing games.

After the conversation, I gave him a letter of reprimand, which notified him that any similar conduct could result in harsher repercussions.

I always make it a point to speak to the employee after this type of encounter within a day or two—see the chart on feedback. This minimizes the tension and accentuates a manager's professionalism. A pleasant greeting or a chat will do the trick.

GROVELING

One other mistake that managers make is to grovel after they have confronted someone.

My former pastor and one of my mentors, Dr. Ron Crum, brought this term to light for me. He explained that often after a confrontation, many leaders attempt to be overly contrite, probably to minimize the feelings of guilt they experience after taking necessary difficult action. I'll admit it, early in my management career, I was guilty of the same behavior.

Stop!

When you confront someone, don't grovel! End the meeting and stay cool, calm, and collected. Move on, and don't allow the seriousness of the situation to be minimized because you feel a need to act apologetic.

By the way, Dean was never a model employee and eventually moved on, but there were certainly no more outbursts. I hope you felt a surge of adrenalin at the thought of you having to confront Dean— not in an unhealthy way—but knowing that if his conduct had been ignored, he would have likely caused further problems which would have contributed to poor morale.

> DL #81: Some people will test your courage in dramatic fashion. Get ready now. Remember, whatever you permit, you promote.

CHAPTER 24: THE OLIVE BRANCH

A great historical event gained recent popularity with the Broadway play *Hamilton*, which tells the story of Alexander Hamilton and Aaron Burr. The two prominent politicians became sore enemies. Hamilton, the former Secretary of the Treasury, began to write letters to his friends about his disdain of Vice President Burr and his policies.

At some point, one of the letters became public, and Burr demanded that Hamilton retract the statements made in the letter. When Hamilton refused, Burr challenged him to a duel. At the duel, history records that Burr shot Hamilton, who died a short time later.

There are two questions that have never been answered:

First, where were the leaders?

And second, how did this conflict continue unabated for so long?

While it has been well documented that both Hamilton and Burr were stubborn, one must wonder what would have happened if John Adams or James Maddison would have conducted a little conflict resolution with the two gents. Maybe they could have conveyed in no uncertain terms that a duel was barbaric and foolish and there were better ways to settle their disagreement.

As with any conflict, it only got worse over time. This story is a tragedy but a great lesson regarding what can happen if conflict is left unchecked.

Don't be naive here. Unless you're trapped on a deserted island, conflict is sure to surface.

The problem with many leaders is that they let conflict fester between employees without addressing it. I get it. Who wants to become involved in what may seem like a petty conflict? For that matter, who wants to get involved in any conflict?

Guess what?

You better get involved and get involved ASAP. If left alone, manager conflicts will likely permeate the team and get worse over time. Then the proverbial duel commences. At that point, it's usually too late. Once employees reach a certain point of contention, there is no turning back.

As I've reiterated, conflict among staff is one of the most difficult situations for managers to address. There are some different schools of thought on the resolution process. If the traditional plan to have the two employees meet in an attempt to rectify the situation doesn't work, here are some things you may want to try.

You need to glean an understanding of the conflict and whether to meet with each person to get an emotional inventory. If you meet with them, listen to understand, and try to stay neutral. Stay focused on the future, not the past, and try to find some middle ground.

At this point, you may have to mediate a meeting with both parties, using similar strategies. This must be done early in the conflict, and hopefully, things will improve.

Many books I've read address this issue and lead one to believe that, after the brilliant manager steps in and administers the ten steps to conflict resolution, everyone hugs, sings Kumbaya, and leaves the office holding hands. Can you see the unicorns and rainbows?

Here's the dirty truth. There are employees who don't trust one another, and they are simply not going to work well together.

There will be times when traditional conflict resolution won't bring about the necessary change that is needed. If that happens, the manager must assert authority and provide both parties with clear expectations and possible repercussions if the issue resurfaces.

Once I had two employees who couldn't get along. At first, I tried to entice them to work together with a good motivational speech about teamwork. This lasted for about two weeks, then the issue resurfaced.

I realized that I needed to handle things differently. We did the lunch thing, and they had discussions that seemed to bring unity. I thought to myself, "This is it. These two are now BFFs." Okay, I'm not that naïve, but I was optimistic.

Yet, true to form, another issue arose. The conflict was regarding workflow and responsibilities. When I met with their direct supervisors about this issue, we agreed to assign work in clear terms to make sure there was no confusion about responsibilities. Again, this helped.

But, you guessed it, it happened again.

At this point, I'd had enough. I called them into my office and explained in no uncertain terms that they must work together when needed or personnel action would be taken. When they started to ask questions or make comments, I refused to yield the floor and asserted that I would do the talking.

After the come-to-Jesus meeting, there were no further conflicts between these two that required my attention. They never hung out on the weekends, but when they had a project to complete, they cooperated enough to avoid any further intervention.

DL #82: Some people just refuse to get along with their peers. In those cases, set boundaries. Manage people, not personalities.

CHAPTER 25: I HAVE MY OWN TRIBE

THE REBEL

Talk with any manager who has several employees, and nearly all will tell you they have that one employee who refuses to be part of the team.

While I have a few stories of my own, there is a story in the Bible that exposes this attitude quite vividly.

The story is about a man named Absalom, the son of the King David who killed Goliath with a slingshot. Absalom was known as the best looking and most popular guy in the kingdom, but he got full of himself and decided to start his own tribe. Absalom became toxic. Basically, when people came to his dad to settle disputes or seek judgment, Absalom would wait down the road and talk with them. He would brag about his own abilities and say that, if he were king, he would dispense judgment far better than his dad had done. He shook a lot of hands and kissed a lot of babies. After a while, he stole the hearts of the people. Sound familiar?

Ultimately, Absalom split the kingdom, and a war ensued. During the battle, Absalom was fleeing from one of his dad's mighty warriors named Joab, when Absalom's horse went through some thickets. He grabbed a tree limb and was hanging in the air. Joab came onto the scene and thrust three spears through Absalom's heart. It was over. But rather than celebrating, David wept at the death of his son.

Dealing with the Absaloms in your company is painful, if you're a compassionate manager.

Every agency, business, organization, and religious institution always has that one person who thinks he or she is smarter and could be a much better leader than the current manager. And if you don't have one now, trust me, eventually you will.

These employees, often insecure, project an image of superiority. They're usually talented, but they have no concept of what it means to be a team player. They want to make themselves look good to a few but will avoid joining the rest of the tribe.

These employees usually begin by criticizing management discreetly, and then more openly. They will also manipulate others and convince them that they're victims, using words to coerce people onto their team such as, "Management is out to get us." Notice the "us."

They usually avoid any extracurricular activities, and they close their door and exhibit other passive-aggressive behaviors. They will dissect emails or statements made at staff meetings and try to find the one sentence they can reengineer to make their point while playing the victim.

These people are toxic and must be controlled and, if possible, removed. The sooner you come to terms with this fact, the better. There are several ways to do this.

First, minimize their platform. In other words, don't give them opportunities to get more exposure and gain more staff support.

Next, if they have a follower or more than one follower—which they always do—don't allow these employees to work together on any project, unless it can't be avoided.

Finally, be very careful when you respond to their complaints in writing. Everything you write, including emails, may be used in a future personnel hearing.

This isn't fun, but many managers have had to deal with this. It's an unfortunate part of the job.

Take Phillip. Philip had an employee named Kurt who was the quintessential rebel. At first, Kurt was tight with Phillip. Then, Philip noticed that Kurt was always in conflict with someone. As long as Philip saw things the way Kurt saw them, everything was fine. But when Philip began to see that Kurt was actually the problem, he addressed Kurt's culpability. Kurt became distant and barely spoke to Phillip, and that was just the beginning.

Phillip attempted to regain a relationship with Kurt by allowing him to take the lead on a project and approved nearly all of Kurt's training requests.

Please listen to this part closely. Phillip's attempt to win Kurt's favor was a mistake. Nothing changed whatsoever. As a matter of fact, it got worse. See, the Kurts of the world want to be in control. They want to be the influencers. As expected, Kurt continued to be a problem for Philip and others until he was finally reprimanded.

I must be honest here. Before I became more astute to human behavior, I would have thought that Phillip's plan to give Kurt more exposure and more accommodations would have brought him back on the team. Experience has taught me better.

While there are situations when people who have gone to the dark side can be restored, it is highly unlikely.

The telltale sign with Kurt was his inability to get along with others and his lack of effort to do so. A good manager must look at all signs of behavior to appropriately address this type of issue. Often, this takes time since these employees don't always do things overtly. They tend to operate on the fringes.

When you have a Kurt in your tribe, it is important to strengthen your tribe and make sure the other wannabe tribe is irrelevant. Don't allow them to affect the mission. If that takes a confrontation, so be it.

Don't back down.

Here are some steps to deal with the rebel. First, talk to him one-on-one on a regular basis and ask direct questions such as, "What did you think about the staff meeting?" And never forget, "Are you getting what you need from me?"

Of course, there are times when they might have a change of heart, but that is rare.

Therefore, to make sure that this cancer doesn't spread further, don't allow them to avoid mandatory meetings, training, etc. Also, make sure they participate in group assignments. Remember, others are watching to see how you handle this situation. If you avoid it, you will have a separate tribe operating within the office, and you will lose the respect of staff.

When the time comes, and the rebel steps over the line, take decisive action. You'll be a superhero to the staff, since you have protected them from Mr. Bully, Negative Nelly, or the Victim Recruiter.

DL #83: There is only one tribe. Either join or leave. As your organization grows, so will the derelicts. Deal with it.

PART VI

FRIENDLY CAUTIONS

A lot of leadership and management material focuses on the "Kumbaya" side of things. And when people get into cautions against prejudice or crossing the line, it's often in very sterile corporate-speak that everyone tunes out.

Straight up, I've seen people lose promising careers over some really stupid stuff that could easily have been avoided.

If you're on the rise in the world, I don't want to see you get derailed. So, call these some friendly cautions. This is table talk stuff, it's not necessary in the Harvard Business Review, but if you pay a little attention, I might be able to save you a world of trouble.

Even if you're on the straight and narrow, you might see someone reporting to you who is on the verge of doing something stupid, and a friendly coffee and table talk might help you save their career. So even if these friendly cautions don't apply to you, they still might help you be a more perceptive and impactful leader.

CHAPTER 26: FRIEND TODAY, BOSS TOMORROW

BFFs

Although we have discussed how to lay the groundwork when you are first promoted, there is one more issue we need to discuss. No one seems to provide guidance for when you get promoted among your peers.

This is one of the more difficult issues to navigate. As a matter of fact, you need to have a plan going into this new role, or you might make some serious mistakes that are difficult or impossible to repair.

I remember the uneasy feeling of competing with colleagues for a promotion, then experiencing an odd reaction when I was selected for the position. It was difficult to adjust accordingly. I wish I'd had a mentor bring me out for coffee and pasta and give me a heads-up and advice. Seriously.

My promotion was announced late on a Friday afternoon, so hardly anyone was around to congratulate me or pretend to be excited I got the job instead of them.

I returned on Monday as the head of the academy. It felt like I had landed on Mars.

It was interesting to watch when people congratulated me. I could literally tell who was authentic and who did it out of obligation.

At first, I believed I needed to project a sense of humility to make sure everyone knew that I was still the same guy. But the truth is, I was not the same guy. They needed a leader. And a leader is not necessarily your friend.

As you navigate the new promotion, you can expect a few different behaviors. Most of these behaviors have been discussed earlier in the book.

There is one category of employee we haven't discussed: the brownnoser. While he or she might inflate your ego—and God knows, it feels good—you must realize that, if you enable this behavior, it will damage the morale of other employees and you will lose the benefit of objective opinions. To help you spot a brownnoser, listen for statements like, "You always do the right thing," "Great job, as always," or, "I was the only one who agreed with you."

After meetings, they often will circle back around to let you know that they agree with you, they will regularly compliment your wisdom, and they will usually criticize others and secretly tell you who is against you. The key to managing these employees is to make sure they're not given special attention or projects. Treat them like every other person and they'll eventually get the hint.

DL #84: Don't allow manipulators to deafen your senses to opposing views. You need staff who will minimize your blind spots.

Back to the promotion. While you may have friends among the ranks, you must realize that your relationship with them will change. The best way to handle this is to be proactive. You must explain to your friends that you have to create some distance to avoid ostracizing other staff. If they are true friends, they will understand the situation.

Of course, you care about them and want them to remain an ally, so don't be so distant that it damages your work relationship. This is a delicate issue, and you're not expected to be harsh or rude. However, if there are times when you wish to socialize with friends or staff, be open about it. It is very detrimental to morale if you are interacting with one or two of your staff and bump into another staff member. Transparency in this case is the best remedy.

In one instance, a person I considered to be a friend began exhibiting poor work performance. I had to call that person in and discuss the issues that had been brought to my attention. The fact that we were friends made this encounter much more difficult.

I could have ignored the issue to make sure that I maintained the friendship, but that would have undermined the mission, and there would not have been any improvement. I addressed the issue, and, frankly, it did strain the friendship. After several months, our relationship began to improve. But, without a doubt, it was never the same again. That is the cost of being a leader.

DL #85: Promotions will alter friendships. Accept it and handle them with a proactive strategy.

CHAPTER 27: MY KINGDOM

THE POWER OF MIDDLE MANAGERS

In this section, there are some things you don't want to do as a middle manager.

Although mid-level managers are not supported in some organizations, in others they wield tremendous power. Unlike senior management, middle managers usually interact with staff daily. A manager's office is a good place for staff to congregate, glean information, and shoot the breeze. Middle managers are in a position of power and can use this time to coach, build vision, encourage staff and show support for other managers. Or, they can use this time to build themselves up in an unhealthy manner, creating their own little fiefdom.

Laura got promoted to acting senior manager in charge of an office. She was very bright, had solid interpersonal skills, and had the ability to be effective in this role. However, there were two middle managers we'll call M&M who had gotten passed over for the same promotion, and they set out on a quest to undermine Laura.

Every time Laura made a decision, M&M manipulated the employees in their respective units. For example, Laura implemented a policy to allow for telework on Fridays. M&M attempted to convince their staff that Laura did that only to make herself look good and that she would use the policy to manipulate them. Any decision she made was met with doubt and suspicion, at least from the more immature employees who were susceptible to this type of thing.

M&M continually undermined Laura's abilities, mocked most of her decisions, and basically convinced some staff that she was on a quest to ruin the agency. They literally destroyed Laura's chances of getting the permanent senior management position. While this may sound ridiculous, it happens all the time. That's right. Some middle managers are somewhat Hitleresk in their approach to controlling behavior.

Here's another example of how middle managers can sway the opinion of their employees. Corporate announces a new policy that requires a monthly in-person staff meeting. The middle manager can support the decision by advising staff that this is a great opportunity for improved communication and will be time well spent. Conversely, middle managers can advise staff that all staff meetings are a waste of time and that upper management is doing this only to exercise more control. Get the picture?

Middle managers with maturity understand that it's vital to support upper management. Also, when middle and senior management support each other, it sends a clear and powerful message to staff. A by-product of unity between middle and upper management is that it will produce an undercurrent of positivity that will likely deter most staff from undermining their managers.

When middle managers have an issue with a senior manager or a corporate directive, they must communicate the issue clearly with their superiors instead of grandstanding their disagreement in front of staff.

DL #86: In some organizations, middle managers are the pendulum of power. Middle managers should use their influence wisely and support one another and senior managers, if possible.

CHAPTER 28: EMBRACING CHANGE

WELCOME TO THE TWENTY-FIRST CENTURY

"This is how we've always done it."

How many times have you heard that tired old phrase? My interpretation of that is "Loser!"

In order to grow and develop as a leader, you must embrace change or be adaptable. Part of this book was written during the Covid-19 pandemic. Managers either experienced defeat or made the necessary adjustments in the way they communicated and conducted business.

Even before the pandemic, let's face it, the world is always changing at what seems to be record pace. People are processing multiple threads of information and are busier than ever. That's one of the reasons podcasts have experienced a resurgence. Think about how often you see people with earbuds in their ears.

People have a thirst for knowledge but need easy access to free up their hands for other things. It is vital for leaders to be versatile and always evolving.

In 2010, I switched from a Blackberry to an iPhone. I came home after work, got the device out of the box, and started messing around with it, but I had no idea how to navigate this new phone that had been heralded to change the world. The functionality was so different and quite confusing. I kept trying to learn the navigation features but started getting frustrated. My daughter, Jansen, who was eleven years old at the time—who, for the record, did not have a phone—saw me struggling and asked, "What's the problem, dad?" I explained my dilemma. She asked if I wanted her to help. I'm thinking to myself, this is adult stuff, sweetheart. But just to humor myself, I handed her the iPhone.

She started navigating that thing like a computer programmer. At this point, my entertainment turned into curiosity. When I realized she knew what she was doing, I told her to slow down so I could learn. She gave me a tutorial on the basics. I was stunned! When I inquired about her tech skills, she said, "I play around with my sister's phone." Play around? Let's get you a job at the Apple Store!

The most significant innovation in my lifetime is certainly technology. We have moved from emails to text messages. Facebook is now considered a platform for older people, and Instagram and other apps such as TikTok have become the new craze for teens and the twenty to thirty age group, and even a little older.

Online shopping is growing at an amazing rate, so managers in retail sales had better be prepared for this evolution or go ahead and hang a going-out-of-business sign. There are apps for everything, cars that drive themselves, and artificial intelligence is probably the next big advancement—buy stock, trust me. None of these developments can be ignored.

Managers must stay abreast of advancements in technology. This is not too difficult since most staff under the age of thirty can probably provide assistance. You need to be ready. I think the pandemic is proof of that.

The other day I was talking with an employee via Skype, and I was trying to add some questions to the agenda for an upcoming staff meeting. He asked if I was willing to share my screen so he could help. My daughter wasn't home to give me a tutorial, so why not give this guy a try? He not only showed me how to set up questions, he showed me several other features that came in quite handy.

OTHER TRENDS

As a leader, you must stay abreast of evidence-based trends and projections. You should never be married to a particular policy, procedure, or tech platform. If you're going to stay on the path of success, you must be very creative in implementing new ideas and creating a climate in which change is embraced instead of detested.

A while back, along with a couple of instructors I developed a national edged-weapon tactics program. I had researched edged weapons for years and was confident this program was the absolute best it could be. When we began teaching the techniques, the students performed exceptionally well.

In their final exam exercise, the students must enter the Room of Doom. As soon as they enter the room, they get attacked. They must perform numerous tactics they have been taught throughout the program, and it gets quite exhausting. Toward the end, one of the instructors attempts to stab them with a polymer knife. We were amazed at how well they were able to protect themselves. Victory!

Years later, a new instructor came on board. He was very skilled in various types of martial arts and Jujitsu. Shortly after he started instructing, I was chatting with Stephanie, the firearms and safety branch chief, and she was giving an overview of some curricula changes her team was working on. Out of the blue, she said, "David is revising the edged-weapon program." What? Did I hear her correctly? He was revising the best edged-weapon program in the country. Confession. I had a conversation with myself that went something like this, "Ron, if you show too much emotion the team will think you are not open to change, so at least give the new program a look."

I put on a supportive face and reviewed the program. Okay. It was good. Really good. I'm not going to admit in writing that it was better, but I supported the changes.

DL #87: Quality managers must embrace change to move the needle forward. If you're standing still while the rest of the world is moving forward, you might as well be walking backward.

CHAPTER 29: HEART VS. BRAIN

EMOTIONAL INTELLIGENCE VS. EMOTIONAL LEADERSHIP

Emotions are natural for any leader, and effective leaders are compassionate, empathetic, and look out for the wellbeing of others. So, don't misunderstand the next part of the discussion as it relates to emotions.

This section addresses those individuals who often succumb to negative emotions that make others uncomfortable and can result in poor decisions that have a negative impact on the company.

I have worked with staff and managers who make decisions based on their intrinsic mood, misguided beliefs, and insecurities. Often, these people are very compassionate and want to do the right thing. However, they allow their emotions to detract from reason.

There is a difference between emotional intelligence and emotional leadership.

An emotional leader tends to make decisions based on their personal feelings about an issue, sometimes despite policy, procedures, or facts.

On the other hand, emotional intelligence is the ability to navigate many variables. This person understands, uses, and manages emotions in positive ways to relieve stress, communicate effectively, empathize with others, overcome challenges, diffuse conflict, and make sound decisions. One of the key ingredients of emotional intelligence is self-awareness.

To the contrary, emotional leaders often lack self-awareness—at least when they are frustrated, afraid, or confused.

Your IQ might help you secure a job, but emotional intelligence will help you be successful.

Determine if someone is an emotional leader by listening carefully. They frequently make statements that invoke their feelings, which are often exaggerated. You might hear statements such as, "I feel like everyone is out to get me," "That new policy is completely absurd," "I am so aggravated with this whole situation," "I'm so aggravated I want to quit," etc., etc.

If you just read the above and recognized some of the elements of being an emotional leader in yourself, don't beat yourself up. You just need a little practice. Along the same lines, if you have someone on your team who makes these types of statements, they will need some coaching.

Once I made edits to a document prepared by a staff member, and he said, "I feel like you don't like me." The document needed the edits, but he took it personally.

These people can often develop an unhealthy relationship with work.

I spoke with a manager who had a procurement specialist who treated the budget like it was his. This can have benefits, but when he was asked to order items or supplies—already approved by management—he acted as though the funds were coming out of his personal checking account. He would ask questions about purchases, such as, "Why do you need that?" Or, "I think this is a waste of money."

Many people who make emotional decisions have difficulty compartmentalizing issues, and they struggle disconnecting from the job. If they are frustrated about a particular issue, they take their frustrations out on the world. The fact that the internet went down for a couple hours shouldn't ruin your weekend.

GET YOUR EMOTIONS IN CHECK

If you tend to lead with too much emotion, you should start to do some exercises to help you make more rational decisions. Remind yourself not to take things so personally, or to allow situations to be overly exacerbated in your mind. Also, don't panic. Issues will eventually pass. The previous decision-making process is beneficial, but here are some specific ways to improve.

Guard your thoughts: Remind yourself this situation is temporary, and the issue probably won't matter next week or next month. Remind yourself this isn't the end of the world.

If possible, talk to a trusted confidant or mentor: If you are upset, angry, etc., seek guidance before you act.

Read that email carefully before sending: Make sure it has factual information without all of the adjectives.

Guard your words: Try to make more factual statements instead of expressing overdramatized emotions. Warning: this is not referring to empathy or assertiveness. There are times when both of those are needed.

Sometimes emotional leaders become self-centered. I worked with an individual once who came to me and said, "When you mentioned timeliness, I felt you were referring to the fact that I was thirty minutes late last week." What? Really? I wanted to say, "Sorry, Sally, you're not the center of my world."

In reality, these people can change their reactions, but—get ready—it will take some time and effort.

To promote success with these types of individuals, you must attempt to establish some level of trust. Ask the person if they trust you to give them some feedback. In most cases you should get an affirmative answer. If they say no, you have a whole other issue on your hands...maybe for another book.

When you provide feedback, the Ward Method can be used, with some slight variation to meet the specific need. During the feedback meeting, be sure to reiterate some specific statements this person has used in the past and explain why those statements were not rooted in fact. This will ideally promote introspection while they are emotionally charged.

For example, I had another employee who made everyone uncomfortable in group meetings by saying, "That hurts," or "You should have known better," to others in the group. When I met with her, I used exact quotes and reiterated the context for which they were used. Then I explained that there must be a free flow of discussion for a meeting to be beneficial. If someone is afraid he or she is going to hurt your feelings or be degraded by you in front of the group, they will shut down.

Next, we discussed why she felt that anyone would intentionally say things to hurt her feelings. She brought up a previous employer and informed me that it had been an abusive work environment.

We then discussed the need for her to take steps to work through those issues and give her new employer and colleagues the benefit of the doubt. She agreed, and the next meeting was much more successful. Of course, I met with her after the meeting and complimented her for her objective approach to the meeting. Always acknowledge improvement.

Never think these individuals will change their mindset after one great coaching session. As with any change of behavior, it takes time.

Your own emotions will not rectify the problem. Watch your vocabulary and your physical responses to statements and situations. If someone has you frustrated, take some breaths, script out your thoughts—which should not reflect your personal feelings but the other person's behavior or impact on the mission—then rehearse and role play. When ready, either meet one-on-one or pick up the phone. You'll be much more respected.

Remember, negative visceral responses not only minimize leadership, they make other people uncomfortable in your presence.

DL #88: Sometimes you have to use your head more than your heart. Decisions made from emotions alone will eventually hinder the mission and diminish respect for the leader.

CHAPTER 30: PREFERENTIAL TREATMENT

One issue that still exists in businesses and agencies throughout the country is various forms of nepotism. There are many reasons for nepotism, and they aren't all bad. For example, a woman with a small business wants to hire her daughter because she knows she can trust her. I get it. However, in large organizations, nepotism can be a real problem.

Rich, a manager friend of mine, oversaw a software sales company and had an opening for someone to sell software in a particular region. His friend, Chad, asked Rich if he would consider hiring his son, Chuck. Chuck had been a local football star and was quite well known in the area. He had a football scholarship to a small college and was expected to be a star. His dreams had been cut short when he tore his ACL and had to undergo surgery. This severe knee injury ended Chuck's football career, so he left college and returned home.

Rich liked Chad's son and had watched him play football. But when he reviewed Chuck's resume, he saw he didn't have any real experience. Even so, Rich overlooked several more qualified applicants and hired Chuck. Rich assigned Gayle, a longtime employee, to help Chuck through the onboarding process and train him to sell software. Shortly after the training started, Gayle reported that Chuck wasn't very observant and struggled with some of the basic functions needed for the job. Rich justified his reasoning for hiring Chuck by telling the other employees that Chuck had excellent interpersonal skills, which would supersede his lack of experience and knowledge.

To Rich's chagrin, he learned that Chuck stayed on his phone, couldn't follow instructions, made numerous mistakes, and hardly made any sales. Soon, Rich's superiors started asking why sales were declining. Rich explained that one of the new employees was not performing. He was told to get rid of the employee and find someone who could do the job. Finally, after months of anguish, Rich had to fire Chuck. And you guessed it. Chad blamed Rich, and said Chuck claimed that no one took time to train him.

Here's the body count: 1) The company lost money, 2) Rich lost a friend, 3) Rich was stressed out, 4) Rich looked bad to his superiors, 5) Rich had to solicit another employee and start the hiring and training process all over again, and, 6) Rich lost the respect of other employees who knew he'd hired his friend's son.

Was it worth it? You tell me.

GOOD OLD BOY NETWORK

There are other forms of nepotism that involve quid pro quo, or I'll scratch your back if you scratch mine. This happens frequently in government and businesses. At the Academy, we invited adjunct instructors from out of town to both instruct and serve as role players. This is a great opportunity for managers and staff throughout the system to get involved. Also, Charleston isn't a bad place to visit!

During the first week after my promotion, I was given a list of visitors, and I noticed the same four people were listed as role players multiple times. When I inquired, I was told that one of these individuals would basically call an administrative staff member at the Academy and direct her to add all four of the manager's names to assist at the same time. You guessed it; they were all pals.

When I found out, I developed an official protocol for adjunct faculty and guest role players. A communication went out, and I removed the Fantastic Four, so they were only allowed to assist on one occasion that year.

When you take a stand against the good old boy network or other forms of nepotism, it might not be popular. Hold firm and operate with integrity. There is a fine line between doing someone a favor and giving them an unfair advantage. Be smart.

DL #89: Don't discriminate or do special favors to give someone an advantage. When hiring staff, select the best candidate for the position. Take an objective look at talent, experience, motivation, education, and values to make sure they fit the company's culture.

CHAPTER 31: CONFIDENTIALITY

IF I TOLD YOU, I WOULD HAVE TO KILL YOU

Confidentiality is a must for an organization to thrive. Everyone expects confidentiality as it pertains to medical records, whistleblowers, or police informants. But it is important in nearly all organizations.

A manager must accept the fact that there will be policies, data, discussions, personnel, and many other issues that cannot be shared.

When I was a USPO, in most cases when the U.S. Attorney's Office planned to file several indictments against a large number of people and numerous arrests were about to take place, the office would notify Pretrial Services of the operation.

Pretrial Services officers are instrumental immediately after the arrests and need to be prepared for the influx of people. Early notification permits Pretrial Services to have enough officers available to interview the people arrested and prepare bail reports.

Imagine the DEA has conducted an investigation on meth distribution for several months. They secured a confidential informant (CI) who was able to gain enough trust to make recorded meth purchases while wearing a body wire to record the transactions. In each instance, agents provided drug money for the purchase and set up surveillance to monitor each transaction. Through other investigative steps, they have compiled a spreadsheet detailing the hierarchy of the illegal operation and most of the significant players. As the investigation continued, they determined the names of the kingpin—the head of the operation—the person cooking the meth, the mules—distributors—and have obtained countless other investigative materials.

Finally, it's time to conduct searches and make arrests. DEA agents divide up into teams and check their tactical gear. They strap on ballistic vests, they make sure their weapons are secure, and they synchronize their watches, so the searches transpire at the same time to prevent someone being tipped off. They travel to the various locations and dozens of arrests are made.

Pretrial Services officers are given a high level of trust to maintain the secrecy of the sting. If this information had been shared outside the agency, it could jeopardize the entire investigation and place the arresting agents in grave danger. Also, if the information leaked, it would damage the relationship between the U.S. Attorney's Office and Pretrial Services, and this type of information might not be shared in the future.

PERSONNEL

Personnel is another sensitive issue that managers must not discuss outside of the management circle of trust.

A manager I knew was dealing with an employee he described as completely incompetent. One day he learned she had made another mistake on a document, so he decided to vent to one of his management friends. He sent an email with the subject, "Another example of incompetence," and attached the document. It would have been a good way to vent, except he hit reply to one of his friend's previous emails, and the troubled employee was included on the thread. I would like to have seen his face when he realized.

The situation was finally rectified, but he was very fortunate that she didn't file an employee dispute resolution complaint.

The bottom line is, one of the dirty sides of management is that confidentiality is sacred and must be protected regardless of the outcome.

> DL #90: Not only will a lack of confidentiality cause staff to lose trust in the manager, it might result in a personnel action.

CHAPTER 32: CROSSING THE LINE

SOCIAL BUTTERFLY

Whether you're an aspiring or a current manager, a real career stopper is hyper-socialization. Hey, I think I just made up a new term! You're welcome. By that I mean when managers feel the need to attend social events with staff and party like a rock-star. Early in my career, I did some socialization. While I never got overly intoxicated, I certainly placed myself in a position that could have potentially gone wrong.

There is nothing wrong with making an appearance at such events. But be warned: Management + excessive alcohol + employees = disaster.

Once, I was at a retirement celebration. A manager we'll call Brady, whom I didn't know that well but had always respected as a professional colleague, had a little—okay, way too much—to drink. Brady was falling all over people, trying to dance.

I remember him hugging me and expressing his undying love for our friendship. He basically made a complete ass of himself. Ordinarily, this might have been funny. But the fact that Brady was among his colleagues did not serve him well. Several people were surprised by his actions, and he is still the butt of several jokes when retirement parties are a topic of discussion.

In another situation, Bruce, a manager, went to a company picnic. It was well-attended, and many staff brought their families. Some groups played team-building games, while others just relaxed and talked. For lunch there were grilled burgers, hotdogs, potato salad, and all the fix-ins. It was a near perfect day.

Bruce and one of his staff members, Phil, and some others started drinking early in the day. Bruce and Chad were very competitive but seemed to enjoy each other's company.

At one point, Bruce, Phil, and a group of employees started playing a friendly game of basketball. Since most of them had been drinking, the trash-talk started getting loud, and few elbows were thrown. Then it happened. Bruce and Phil got into a fight. Although it was broken up quickly without any real physical damage, nearly all of the other employees witnessed the fight and heard the expletives exchanged between Bruce and Phil. Things eventually settled down and both apologized, but the damage had been done. They had ruined the rest of the picnic for everyone.

When managers have to attend a social event, they should never get the least bit intoxicated. In fact, it's best to leave before other staff get hammered and say or do things beyond the manager's control.

DL #91: Managers will never gain respect when they model inappropriate behavior.

FISHING IN THE COMPANY POND

Uncomfortable but true. Occasionally there are employees who develop an unhealthy attraction to their boss. This could be just a fantasy on their part, or maybe they believe a more amorous relationship would bring them success.

The human attraction to confidence and power can cause people to do strange things. Some managers recognize this power and use it in unhealthy ways. Remember, even if it's consensual, it's still a form of manipulation.

From government to corporations to churches, manipulative situations play out every day between managers and staff. It comes in many forms, including assistance outside of work, inappropriate statements, sexual favors, or downright sexual assault.

While the more explicitly sexual side is getting more attention nationally, especially after Harvey Weinstein, you have to realize that misuse of your authority can happen even in more seemingly innocent contexts.

For example, I moved into a new home and needed to paint some rooms. One of my employees offered to paint the rooms for me. While I was grateful, I declined due to the appearance of impropriety.

Another step that I recommend is creating boundaries between your personal and professional life. While it might seem hardcore, I blocked staff from my social media accounts, as I don't believe that we need that level of intimacy. Besides, I didn't really want to see what they had for dinner last night or watch their cat videos.

Back to attraction. When I was a deputy sheriff fresh out of college, I had to ride with various other deputies as part of my onboarding. This was an interesting experience, to say the least. Observing the various personalities and approaches to the job was eye opening.

One officer stands out among the others but not in a good way. He was married but explained to me how women loved men in uniform, as it represented power. He referred to his uniform as a chick magnet.

As we made our rounds, we would stop at different businesses or grab a coffee. It was quite obvious who his conquests were. He was sleeping with three or four women in the town. True, he was a dirtbag, but I quickly realized that he was spot on regarding the attraction to power.

When I was in uniform, it seemed as though people were mesmerized and felt the need to talk to me. It was rare to eat lunch and not be interrupted. Either people would send their child over to speak with me, or they would mention their cousin Ted, a police officer in California, and wanted to see if I knew him. Yeah, Ted and I had lunch the other day, lady.

There are many reasons why some in authority give in to this temptation and risk everything, but I won't do a psychological deep dive. I would note, however, that many managers had never been the object of attraction until they got promoted, so they were simply not prepared to handle this newfound attention.

Before you get too self-righteous, understand that no one is perfect, and sometimes initial temptation is quite subtle. It starts with a thought that grows over time. Think about it. Most people put on their best face at the office. They dress nicely, they act and talk in a professional manner, and they may give their boss compliments that he or she might not get at home. The whole situation begins to grow, the conversations get personal, the passion seeps in. And, before you know it, they're fishing in the company pond. I'll stop here since this isn't *Fifty Shades*.

The bottom line is, as a manager, you'll have many opportunities to abuse your authority. You must understand that doing so is a career-ending decision. Draw a line in the sand and stop this type of situation from the outset and seek guidance from a mentor. In the long run, you'll be glad you did.

DL #92: When tempted, consider the long-term effects of your actions. Finding someone you trust to hold you accountable may be the extra encouragement you need to keep a barrier between your personal and professional life.

I HEARD IT THROUGH THE GRAPEVINE

As mentioned above, confidentiality is a sensitive issue in most organizations, as many aspects of the job require discretion. Secrecy can be difficult since some of the information might be tantalizing, and it's tempting to share. Inquiring minds want to know, right? Some information is routine, such as a manager receiving a call to verify employment when someone is buying a house. Other situations are just plain juicy.

For example, I once received a call from an angry spouse who told me her husband had been cheating and wanted me to do something about it. Her husband worked for me, but his extramarital activities weren't work-related. So, I wasn't sure what to do. One thing is for sure, I was tempted to share this juicy information with other managers. Okay. I was dying to share it. It was difficult, but I kept the information to myself.

Honestly, you wouldn't believe everything that has been brought to my attention in private. When I first got promoted to academy director, managers would call me from either my agency or another agency to let me know who was sleeping with whom, who had a drinking problem, who was getting a divorce, etc. It was good stuff for sure, but when people share gossip with you, no matter how tantalizing, you should show little interest or tell them you're not interested. This is difficult. But, in time, the gossip train will head in another direction.

Throughout my career, I worked with some supervisors who were known to spread gossip and others who were like steel traps. Which of the two groups do you think was more respected? That's right, the supervisors who refrained from gossip.

Actually, I believe gossip is a form of insecurity. People want attention. So, often they will share intimate details at someone else's expense. Remember those friends in high school, or maybe even a current colleague, that you wouldn't dare tell something sensitive because you knew they would spread the information like poison ivy. I'll bet you could name a few right now.

One reason I went beyond confidentiality and added a gossip chapter to this book is because, frankly, I struggled in this area, and I think other managers do as well—maybe you're one of them. I'm not proud of that fact, but I've improved significantly in this area.

Here's the way gossip usually plays out. First someone comes to you, and there's the gossip foreplay. They say, "I heard some interesting news, but I probably shouldn't tell anyone."

You take the bait and assure them your lips are sealed. So, they go one step further and make you absolutely promise not to repeat this tantalizing piece of information. You pinky swear. They make you feel special by saying, "You're the only person I'm sharing this with." Really? Doubt it. Someone else will get the same gossip within twenty minutes.

Here's the dirty truth: After a series of events dating back to high school, I realized that I needed growth in this area. I had gossiped in high school about various things, but the worst was talking about girls who did and girls who didn't. Sometimes I didn't even know for sure. But it was fun and exciting to be the owner and conduit of this sensitive information.

As an adult, in my police career, I found out that one of the deputies was having an affair. Of course, it was juicy, so I told a couple of other deputies. Eventually, the news got back to his wife. When the list of gossipers was revealed, my name came up. I have no sympathy for the cheater, but I was severely embarrassed that I had been part of the gossip trail.

For most people, the ability to withhold private information takes some work. Start somewhere. When you hear any form of gossip and can't avoid it, commit to yourself that you WILL NOT share the information. As you do this, it will get easier. Soon you will begin to feel a sense of pride that you can maintain confidentiality.

DL #93: Not only does gossip harm others, it tarnishes the reputation and integrity of the gossiper. There are ways to get attention without hurting others.

PART VII

PLAYING TO WIN

And so, we begin our last round of learning.

What a journey. I'm going to miss this.

You know what? I appreciate you taking the time to learn from me.

I wish I'd had more information and been more prepared when I became a manager. It was a different era. Now there's a lot more good information. The problem is that many people don't want to make the commitment to learn, grow, and get better.

I appreciate you learning from my lessons and I hope you can make them your own, so you've got a stronger team, a stronger organization, and just maybe a stronger life.

You can practice all these skills. Nobody is born with all of them. You learn on the job and you learn from people you trust. Hopefully, you pass the lessons on.

All right let's talk about how to *win*.

CHAPTER 33: DEDICATION

You know, there's one thing I'm not sure I got clear in our dialogue. When I talk about practicing courage, setting high standards, leading, I'm not just talking about things you do.

You don't just "do" courage. You become courageous.

You don't just "do" high standards because they're written down in a document. You become high standards.

There was a unique and special day of my life I'll never forget. The lesson stuck with me forever. At the time, I was a senior U.S. probation officer and I was the training coordinator. Part of my job was making sure all officers received a minimum of forty hours of annual training.

Dr. Sam Samples was a mentor to me. He wasn't just doing exceptional management or leadership on the job; he really became management. He didn't turn it on and off, it just became part of him.

I remember the day vividly. It was Dr. Sample's final day before retirement. I was apprehensive about the new administration and was sad to see Dr. Samples leave.

Dr. Samples knocked on my door.

I invited him in, and we chatted for a few minutes.

Then he asked me to check to see if he had met the forty-hour training requirement.

I pulled up the records and he had completed— Uh-oh, thirty-eight hours.

I was shocked! What should I say? It was his last day, for God's sake. Should I lie? I just couldn't do it. I glanced up and said, "You have thirty-eight hours."

And then—this burned into my memory—Dr. Samples asked if we had any training videos that could be used to meet the requirement.

We walked together to the area where we kept training videos and selected a couple of one-hour videos.

He took them and went into the conference room.

About an hour later, I walked down the hallway and there he sat, watching the videos. It showed incredible integrity and commitment.

After a while he returned the videos, I added two hours to his training record and assured him that he had now met the requirement.

He was still teaching me on his last day at work. Not because he decided to act with commitment and integrity on that one specific day. He had practiced integrity and commitment for so long, it had simply become who he was.

That's the standard we should all aim for.

CHAPTER 34: TO LEAD WELL, YOU MUST BE WELL

WHEN IT GOES FROM BAD TO WORSE

Beginning in 2012, I started having serious marital problems. Between 2012 and 2015, my wife and I separated twice and, ultimately, divorced.

Things got even worse in 2016. At the beginning of the year, I had a long bout with bronchitis and was involved in a very difficult personnel issue that lasted for almost a year. This issue was both professionally and emotionally draining. In early March, 2016, the divorce was finalized. While I was relieved, there was still an odd, almost eerie feeling. It was finally over.

At the end of March on Good Friday, we had a new officer graduation ceremony at the Academy. This is a big event that airs nationwide within our government TV network. That allows family and friends of the graduates to watch the graduation online in their local federal courthouse, or the graduates can access it on demand upon their return home.

On this particular day, I skipped my morning breakfast shake, thinking that I would grab a bite when I got to work. However, right after I got to my office, some dignitaries arrived early and stopped by to say hello before the ceremony. Between chatting with them and getting my things together to lead the ceremony, I still hadn't eaten.

After the ceremony, I had to attend a lengthy confidential meeting, still on an empty stomach. After the three hour meeting, I was walking to my car, thinking about food and Ibuprofen, when I received a phone call. The person on the other end informed me that my daughter, Haley, had been in an automobile accident and was trapped in her car.

I felt like everything started moving in slow motion. This was every parent's nightmare.

Since my daughter was in and out of consciousness, they attempted to put the phone to her ear so she could hear my voice as they were getting the jaws of life ready to free her from the car.

At that moment, Haley made a gut-wrenching statement. I heard her say, "I can't feel my legs."

My heart sank even further. And to make matters worse, I was about twenty miles away from the accident. I jumped in my car and sped toward the scene. It was by the grace of God that I didn't crash as I weaved in and out of traffic. By the time I arrived, they had removed her from the vehicle, placed her in the ambulance, and were headed to the hospital. I did an immediate U-turn and headed that way.

I still had not eaten and had a pounding headache. By the time I arrived, Haley had received an assessment from one of the emergency room doctors. They would have to x-ray her pelvic area, and she had a collapsed lung and at least one broken rib. It turned out that her pelvis was broken in four places, she had a broken rib, and they had difficulty draining the fluid from the collapsed lung. This was so traumatic that it's still difficult to write about.

I do remember all the love, prayers, and support we received from family and friends. My branch chiefs at the Academy, MJ Gagnon-Odom and Gene DiMaria, were not only at the hospital when Haley was first admitted, they took over some of my work duties so I could spend time with Haley and take care of other family matters. My supervisor, Nancy Beatty in the DC Office, called several times to check on Haley and me, and conveyed her support and well wishes throughout this traumatic event. I am forever grateful for all of their support.

The surgery required special equipment, so Haley was administered morphine for several days. As you can imagine, with my previous job as a USPO, I was deeply concerned about the morphine because of its addictive qualities. After three days, she underwent major surgery. Then the recovery process began. After a few more days in the hospital, she came home in a wheelchair, but amazingly, she was walking within a few days.

As a side-note, the doctor said she wouldn't be able to exercise or jog until December. Nonetheless, against the odds, in September she called and asked me to run a 5K race with her.

I couldn't believe what I was hearing. Was she serious? She was so serious she did what any good daughter would do in this situation, she borrowed my credit card to pay for the race.

On a beautiful day in September, Haley and I ran a 5K. She was in pain the last 200 yards or so and started to cry. But since the doctor had cleared her to run, I pushed her to keep going and we finished the race together.

Who would have believed that a girl who almost lost her life in a terrible crash and came home in a wheelchair, would be able to finish a 5K race six months later?

One of my most prized possessions is a picture of us crossing that finish line.

MOMENT-BY-MOMENT

On a personal level, after Haley's accident, the aggregate stress I experienced was immense. Once again, I began to lose sleep. Between the accident, the difficult personnel issue, taking care of my youngest daughter, Jansen, who lived with me—who has since traveled the world doing missions work—and my already demanding work schedule, I felt like I was spiraling down a bottomless pit.

Netflix became my BFF. That helped some, but I continued to feel as though darkness was closing in around me.

At work, my workout partner, at the Federal Law Enforcement Training Center, Al Hawkins and I had a routine. We would meet around noon to start the day's activities. During this difficult time, I remember sitting at my desk watching the clock and dreading every minute until I had to get dressed to go for a run, practice martial arts, or do CrossFit.

When you're in this deep a state of mental darkness, coupled with no sleep, you dread everything.

Of course, it affected my work as well. It was difficult to make clear decisions, and my daily work responsibilities seemed insurmountable. I had difficulty focusing on the smallest of tasks. And naturally, I did my best to keep all of this to myself instead of seeking help.

There were several days when I should have taken leave. But instead, I plowed through.

Although there were no fatal decisions, had I rested for a day, my decisions and their results would most likely have improved.

I've learned that wellness doesn't occur day by day, but moment by moment. It's the small instantaneous decisions that make a difference.

For example, if you decide to exercise, the decision to get started happens in a moment. You either do it or you don't. If a full day passes and no productive exercise has been accomplished, usually we tell ourselves in that moment, "I'll work out tomorrow."

After several months of barely surviving, I saw a doctor and was prescribed medication to help me sleep. Don't ever denigrate an employee for seeking help. As a matter of fact, encourage it, and applaud it.

Sleeping helped to some extent. Next, I had to take the advice I had given others and try to control all of the turmoil playing out in my mind.

Based on some good advice, I sought out a few activities that I enjoyed. I started playing the guitar again, returned to teaching kickboxing, and started to spend more time with positive people. I saw a counselor briefly and had some long conversations with my mother and my sister, Becky, with whom I could be vulnerable. Never underestimate the power of friends and family when you are in crisis.

In short, I developed a healthier lifestyle. But don't be mistaken, this was difficult. When you're depressed, you lack the drive to get healthy.

The dirty truth is that managers may function for several years before the cumulative stress takes its toll. When it does, however, the results can be dangerous or even fatal.

If you haven't already, please, please establish a wellness plan.

There are thousands of websites and Apps that can help you develop one. You can hire a wellness coach, reach out to your employee assistance program, or find out what other agencies are doing. This is paramount because none of the finer points of management are relevant if you're not healthy. If you don't have a wellness plan, develop one now.

> DL #94: Good managers have a wellness plan that becomes habitual. It should include some form of diet, exercise, a fun hobby, and time with family and friends. These managers recognize that resilience is the key to true success.

HEALTHY MANAGERS MAKE FOR HEALTHY ORGANIZATIONS

As fate would have it, after I got well, I began to oversee the U.S. Probation and Pretrial National Wellness Committee.

At first, I placed a good deal of focus on the wellness of staff, but I quickly realized that managers were hurting as well. Never, ever forget, managers need support as much as staff. Many great managers put their staff first but neglect their own wellness.

In one instance, a U.S. probation officer had to be placed in FBI protective custody due to threats from the Aryan brotherhood. When I called the chief U.S. probation officer, she began to tell me everything she had done to take care of the officer. However, I interrupted and advised her that I already knew the steps that had been taken. I explained that I was calling to check on her. She seemed a little taken aback, but then she began to decompress. We were on the phone for about an hour and it seemed to help her immensely.

After that, I went on a quest. I developed a wellness teaching presentation, and not only did I have the opportunity to make presentations to U.S. probation and pretrial officers throughout the country, I was also a guest presenter at both the East and West coast chief's and deputy chief's conferences. Of all my presentations, this one was the most appreciated.

I later went on to develop a wellness for managers program, too, because I see that group neglected so often. The great managers and leaders of teams are always looking out for the wellness of their staff, but they're often not focusing on their own.

If you're not taking care of yourself, you're not going to be able to take care of others to the best of your ability. That's a fact and you know it. Take your own wellness seriously. Please.

I see a lot of managers think it's weak to set aside time for health-related activities. I know I didn't rest and recover like I should have during that tough time, and the consequences could have been really bad. Frankly, I got lucky.

Many agencies and companies allow administrative leave for a few hours per week for fitness or other health-related programs. Others have office activities such as chair yoga, and some have weight-loss challenges. Take advantage of those.

Don't forget, managers should model wellness by participating. Agencies that have wellness programs reap great benefits. Most agencies report improved staff morale, employees and managers taking fewer sick days, and the company experiencing increased productivity.

Playing to win doesn't mean burning out your health, family, friends, and enjoyment. Just the opposite. You've got to be healthy, connected, and enjoy your life to be the best leader for your team and organization.

If you haven't already, get that program started.

DL #95: Never underestimate stress in the workplace. Management and staff wellness should be promoted in creative ways. The benefits are proven, and the overall health will create a higher level of production and minimize the need for sick leave. It may also save someone's life.

CHAPTER 35: VICTORY DANCE

PEOPLE LOVE TO WIN

One afternoon in 2019, I happened to be in Virginia making a wellness presentation to managers. The night before, the Virginia Cavaliers had just won the NCAA National Basketball Championship. I was in an Uber headed to the airport and the streets were lined with fans, shouting, waving, holding banners, and some were in their cars blowing their horns.

At that moment, the Uber driver yelled, "There they are!"

The buses carrying the players were approaching. It was total pandemonium in the streets. I grabbed my phone and shot a quick video. I had attended basketball camps there, which made it even more memorable.

There is nothing better than winning. The problem is that winning is usually only associated with sports. Most people arrive at work with a dead look in their eyes, push the proverbial timeclock, do their mundane jobs, and leave, thinking they survived another day. But maybe they are the walking dead.

Because they never experience a win.

Again: They never experience a win.

One small business owner told me he didn't want staff to know when sales were up because they might expect a raise. Really? His staff doesn't get the pleasure of knowing that business is good? That explained the dead look in many employees' eyes.

Other than sales, many agencies have no concrete way to measure success. Often, employees will finish a difficult task, or a team will finish a project only to be given another one. They might hear a manager say, "Good job," and that's about it.

In places like that, the team never gets to experience a win. These businesses, organizations, and agencies don't have any proverbial finish lines; therefore, they don't see the prize or experience the thrill of victory.

As a matter of fact, a lot of organizations never encourage their employees to thrive at all. They accept mediocrity and operate in survival mode.

It is paramount that staff know when they win. It doesn't have to be a national championship, it can be a project, or even as simple as a positive meeting. You must clearly identify what winning means, provide encouragement and strategies to win, and don't forget to promote victory celebrations.

To do so, you must set realistic goals within your team and challenge each employee to contribute to reach those goals. And then, make sure your team gets to experience the win.

I knew one manager who was involved in sales and used a large thermometer that he built at home. Yes, he could have used an electronic one but wanted staff to see how serious he was about the goal. Every time sales increased, or the team brought in potential customers, he would draw a line on that thermometer noting the increase. That visualization helped motivate staff, and sales continued to rise. Of course, when victory was attained, he found ways to celebrate, and then came up with a new idea.

I'll say it again: In many organizations, the team never gets to experience a win.

The key word is experience.

Experience.

DL #96: Take the time to find ways to get your team to experience the win when it happens. It's enjoyable. It's amazing for morale, service, and teamwork. It gets addictive.

SMALL EXPERIENCES OF WINNING ADD UP

Things that may seem insignificant can go a very long way with staff. I wish I'd learned that earlier, because it's incredibly powerful and good for everyone.

During a recent government shutdown due to a funding gap, our agency continued to operate. One day, I received a call from Lee Ann Bennett, Deputy Director of the Administrative Office of the U.S. Courts.

She had previously visited the Academy and displayed great interest in our mission. She was calling to check on our staff and asked if there was anything she or headquarters could do in the way of assistance.

A few day later, she sent a stack of personalized cards for every staff member.

Her phone call and cards meant a great deal to me and the staff.

At the Academy we did a weekly update and one of the biggest hits was "pic of the week." These photos featured various staff members. Some were funny and some were showcasing staff talents. After a while, staff started sending me pics to be featured.

Another great tool we developed were fifty-nine-minute cards. Basically, if someone superseded expectations, their supervisor could give them a fifty-nine-minute card, which permitted them to leave fifty-nine minutes early anytime they chose, within certain guidelines.

At one point, an employee bought a plastic name tent that read, "I'm kind of a big deal." He put it on my desk as a joke, and I loved it.

I decided to make it an actual award. This award would be given to a staff member each week for superior contributions. The best part was, the recipient would be determined by his or her colleagues. The winner would keep the award in their office for a week and then it was passed onto the next recipient. We also took a picture of the winner for the weekly update.

When employees excelled in a particular function, I tried to find the time to write handwritten thank you cards.

A handwritten note not only expresses intimate appreciation, it creates a positive reflection on you as a leader.

> DL #97: Give employees some individual victories, whether in-person or via video conference, phone calls, or a hand-written note. It will go a long way

OTHER AWARDS

Fortunately, our agency allowed for three separate hundred-dollar bonus gift cards per year. When employees went above and beyond, I made the effort to get them a gift card.

Never underestimate the power of phone calls, stopping by someone's office to say thank you, or a letter to their personnel file. These things will help solidify a positive culture. The gestures may sound simple, but they will go a long way with your staff.

In many "walking dead" organizations, the team never gets to experience a win.

Start letting them experience it. Make it real. There's always more service to perform and more work to do, but the experience of winning refuels and recharges like nothing else.

It might sound funny, but some people may never have learned how to win. Can one practice celebrating and experiencing winning? Like anything else, you sure can.

There are many ways to motivate the team and celebrate accomplishments. Be creative. Winning is addictive!

UNDEFEATED

I love cheerleaders. Hold on, there's a valid reason. I was at a high school football game, and one team was getting destroyed. Do you think that affected the nature of the cheers?

No!

If you were not watching the game and only listening to the cheerleaders, you would have thought the losing team was winning by a landslide. It's all right, it's okay, we're gonna beat them anyway!

Yes, you will have to address dirty issues. However, always step up to the plate with the belief that you are going to hit a homerun. Strive to end every day, every meeting, every project, undefeated.

When leaders eat, sleep, and breathe victory, they create a culture of winning. In time, staff will either get on board, feel out a place, or move on. Any of these three dynamics is a win for the manager and the organization.

Some managers have told me their organization's culture is just bad and it's too late to turn things around. Never accept this ideology. It may take time, but things can and will change with a winning strategy.

If you wind up in a situation where the team or organization isn't doing well—it's not uncommon for successful managers to be promoted into tough situations like that—pretend it's halftime and your team is beat up, sweaty, tired, and a couple are injured. What would you say to this team?

I don't think you would say, "We blew it but there's always next year." No, you would devise a winning strategy and deliver the motivational speech of a lifetime.

DL #98: Always remind the team that setbacks are temporary, but a winning attitude is permanent.

STEPS TO VICTORY

At the Academy where I served, our vision was to provide the absolute best training possible to our federal officers while upholding the honor and integrity of the federal judiciary.

To fulfill our mission, we implemented skill-enhancement training so our instructors could hone their skills and continue to improve. I reminded them to bring their A-game to every session.

We also promoted continuing education, reviewed student feedback, acknowledged excellent conduct with gift cards, and I, along with other managers, always shared praise from stakeholders, senior executives, and federal judges.

Thankfully, almost all of the feedback was favorable. Touchdown! Then we had staff celebrations. Sometimes a victory dance in the end zone is needed. On the off chance the feedback was negative, we dealt with it.

For years, I told our instructors they were the best our system had to offer. I had some managers ask me why I continued to say that when we had some poor performers. I explained that while everyone on the team wasn't Michael Jordan, if we could get those team members to believe they were on a winning team, they were more likely to take their abilities to the next level.

DL #99: As soon as you can, head into the locker room at your company and get your team started on the path to victory.

PART VIII

FULL CIRCLE

I'm lying in bed; my mind is racing. I just can't get comfortable. I look at my phone—midnight. If ever I've needed a good night's sleep, it's tonight. At 9:30 tomorrow morning, I have to terminate a tenured employee who falsified timesheets. It's my job to drop the anvil. Lucky me. I turn on the light and try to read with little success, then I try again. Finally, I fall asleep around 2:00 a.m. After what seems like fifteen minutes, the alarm goes off.

Ugh! I hate that sound.

It's 5:30 a.m. I get up, shower, make my health shake, drink some coffee. Put on one of my best suits—have to dress the part.

Morning commute. Arrive at my office at 7:15 a.m.

And wait.

Finally, 9:00 a.m. I'm exhausted—the kind of exhaustion where it takes too much energy to even determine how I feel. Thirty minutes and counting.

It had taken me and two other managers numerous hours over three days to connect the dots. In matters like these, a specific itinerary must be in place that includes sharing the investigation with senior management, seeking guidance from the internal legal office, conducting a conference with human resources, and arranging for a security officer to be in the office next to mine—you can't be too careful in today's world.

The emergency signal is in place to notify security in case things turn ugly. Security officials are on standby, also waiting for him to arrive. There are cardboard boxes hidden in the adjacent office waiting for him so that he can collect his personal belongings and, hopefully, expedite his exit from the premises.

Tick-tock. The clock in my office reminds me how slowly seconds can pass in times like these. Every minute that passes feels like a minor panic attack.

My mind is racing. I feel a tension headache coming on. I'm not sure if Tylenol or a morphine drip would better serve me. I try to remember strategies from the superfluous motivational/leadership books I've read over the years, as if by the grace of God, some lightning bolt of pliable information will magically surface from the depths of my brain. But it would seem that, credible though they are, those books didn't provide me with the direction and courage I need to muster by 9:30 a.m.

Then it starts: The self-doubt creeps in like a crazy ex-girlfriend who just discovered my new cell number. I start to question myself and my conduct over the years: *Had I ever lied? Or bent the rules?* I mean, I'm no saint, and I'm about to alter the course of this guy's life—his future, his family's future.

I become acutely aware of the lump in the back of my throat. My mouth feels as dry as the Sahara Desert. It becomes hard to swallow.

At first, my big promotion looked sexy. The big office, the chance to influence the agency, travel, a generous pay raise. What's not to love? But now, none of that seems to matter.

It's 9:10. I skim through my notes one last time. I feel my heart beating; my hands are slightly trembling like the day after a night of binge-drinking.

I receive word that he has arrived and is sitting in his car. Waiting.

What must he be thinking right now? Will he admit to his conduct? Will he think I'm the biggest jerk on the planet? What if he appeals, forcing management into a long, drawn out cat and mouse game? No. We need this to end quickly so we can backfill his position. We are short-staffed as it is. *Please God.*

Hopefully it will be over in just a few minutes. After all, what are a few minutes compared to an entire lifetime?

Okay, Ron, focus. You've got this. I knew at some point I would have to do something like this—I just didn't think it would be this soon.

Okay. 9:20 a.m. *Deep breath.* I put an HR rep on speaker phone and ask another manager to be present as a witness.

Tap-tap-tap. A brisk knock on the door.

Showtime.

SHOWTIME...

You may be wondering how my meeting went with Tyler.

The purpose of this meeting was to terminate him. And I'm not exaggerating how much it ate at me, how I second-guessed myself, how nervous I was.

All of us have been there. These things tend not to be written about in books on management but talk to any manager about the first time they had to do something like that. It can be seriously intense.

You want to know how it went with me?

Here it is in one word: Anticlimactic.

Tyler knocked on the door, the other manager and I shook his hand. I asked him to take a seat.

I positioned him so the other manager had access to the door, if needed. Remember, most of our staff were firearms and defensive tactics instructors. I mustered the courage to let him know what our investigation had concluded. I took a deep but discrete breath as I described his alleged misconduct. I think my voice might have cracked a little, but hopefully it wasn't too noticeable. Tyler became emotional and admitted to the misconduct with a long, teary-eyed apology.

To my relief, it was over quickly.

Shortly after, the meeting ended, and I had to accompany him as he collected his office equipment. I confiscated his phone, computer, and other items. Needless to say, our conversation was extremely awkward. He gathered his things, and I walked him to his car. A few minutes later, security advised that Tyler had left the campus. It was finally over.

While I certainly empathized with him, I felt such relief. Whether it was the investigation or the meeting itself, afterward I was completely deflated.

Even though the meeting was somewhat uneventful, I remember telling myself that I would never succumb to this level of stress again. And I haven't.

If you've been on the job decades now, you know what that kind of stress is like. But if you're new, you've now been given the basic strategies to prepare yourself.

Since that day, I've had numerous encounters that required feedback, from suspensions to terminations. But be assured, after practicing and building up my courage and skills, these encounters were much easier.

I still have compassion for the people involved, but I have no problem with confrontation when it is needed. And with practice, you won't either.

Take it from me, I've seen a lot of different walks of life. You can develop resiliency, courage, empathy, and control in all kinds of situations that you might have never dreamed you'd experience. And in your path of leadership, you will.

DL #100: Leave it better than you found it!

ONE LAST CUPPA JOE

I never thought I'd be here.

I still ask myself how it happened. The little guy growing up in a very rural area where aspirations were often limited and resources few.

Yet, somehow, I held onto a dream and began to realize that goals are attainable, the human spirit is limitless, and hard work knows no bounds.

As we complete our journey, I want to leave you with some parting advice. Never limit yourself by the words of others or the circumstances you face. My sincere desire is that you will make the most of your own journey and keep the faith in those difficult times. Never let fear hold you in its grip but use the lessons you have learned to become a courageous leader and bring about positive change in your organization and the people you serve.

Greet every day as an adventure and a chance to grow. Surround yourself with positive people to help mold and shape you, so you, in turn, can do the same for the next up-and-coming group of leaders.

Here is a challenge: Never accept normal. Never accept average. Great leaders have never been characterized as normal or average. They are extraordinary. It doesn't matter the position you hold. Whether you serve at a church, a small business, or a Fortune 500 company, greatness is an attitude. It is a combination of lofty goals, hard work, a desire to serve others, and the fortitude to never give up.

I have not arrived, but I have evolved. I try to seize opportunities with a hunger that can only be curbed by greeting the next adventure. I have been blessed beyond measure. How did this happen? I wish I had all of the answers, but we can never see the end from the beginning. What I have come to understand is that human beings have great potential, and we're only limited by the barriers we often build in our own consciousness. Some say I am a leader; some might disagree. I am not defined by either.

My desire is, and has always been, to grow and improve. With this as a compass, I remind myself that new horizons await, and with God's guidance, I must be the pioneer of my destiny. If I can help others pursue their destiny, bring hope and enlightenment to mankind, and leave a legacy of hope and sublime, I have won the battle.

For you, I am grateful. Grateful to have shared this journey with you. Grateful for your next chapter. Grateful that you will most certainly develop into a leader of character, courage, and conviction.

NOW GO FORTH AND CONQUER

Yes, this has been quite a journey. Thank you for taking time to read the pages of my life and allowing me to provide guidance to help you develop into the leader you are meant to be. If one day your life is a story, what will your story be? You are the author. Each page depends on your decisions, your actions, and your pursuit of greatness.

As your story progresses, I charge you to use your life experiences and the lessons we've explored together to be a courageous leader, working for the betterment of others and your organization.

Don't you dare have a chapter in your story that is average. Commit at this moment to become a lifelong learner, practice, improve, conquer.

Be a leader who never looks back but looks forward, always pursuing a dream.

Never let your circumstances or past failures determine your future triumphs.

Your story will involve hard work.

Courage.

Sometimes it will be lonely. Sometimes thankless.

But you know who you are.

You know who you want to become.

Because of your commitment to lead, bullies will be defeated, lives will be enriched, people will excel, and your family, your staff, and your organization will be extraordinary.

Now it's time.

People are crying out for leaders.

Listen, they're calling your name.

Lead.

THE END (FOR NOW)

PS:

I plan to devote the next phase of my life to helping managers and leaders be prepared for the many challenges that are sure to come. That is why I formed 4Ward Management Coaching. I want to make a difference and never see other managers having to suffer through many of the struggles I had in the beginning of my own management career.

Throughout history, great leaders have risen up during challenging times. The international workforce is advancing, and technology continues to be at the forefront of nearly everything we do. Regardless of the changes in society or in your agency, one thing is certain: Courageous leadership is the key to success.

For speaking engagements, management training and consulting, and other online resources for leaders, visit Ronward.com.

DIRTY LESSONS AT A GLANCE

DL #1: If you don't have a Plan B, C, and D, Plan A may leave you in a lurch. Solid managers build a web of alternate plans.

DL #2: If you are not serving, you're not leading. Make service a part of everything you do.

DL #3: Be patient with the progress of new employees. Effective onboarding requires time and patience.

DL #4: Don't be afraid to question company policies or programs that are outdated or seem to serve no purpose. If it has no value, change it.

DL #5: Never withhold important information from your superiors. This will damage trust, minimize your influence, and might even get you fired.

DL #6: Effective leaders strive for greatness and do not allow small thinkers to obstruct their pursuit.

DL#7: Always examine the reasons behind your actions. If it's solely to impress someone, don't do it!

DL #8: Stand up to bullies in your organization. There will always be those who don't play well with others, and they must be dealt with.

DL #9: There are times when you must trust the process and the decision maker. Assume positive intent instead of malice.

DL #10: Cultivate a workplace culture where new ideas are welcomed and heard. Sometimes our greatest brilliance is found when we step away from routine.

DL #11: Mishandling finances is one of the biggest mistakes a manager can make. Make sure you and your team understand the ethics and policies for use of company resources.

DL #12: Staff your weaknesses, as you don't want to be surrounded with those employees who are just like you. Diversity brings strength.

DL #13: There are situations when corporate or headquarters may not provide the support you need. This does not relieve you from doing what is right, even if you're flying solo.

DL# 14: Understand staff personalities and their possible journeys before you react too harshly. The more a manager understands his or her employees, the more effective he or she can be in coaching the individual.

DL #15: The tallest trees catch the most wind. Leadership can make you a target.

DL #16: Build on your strengths and minimize your personal weaknesses. Never stop investing in yourself.

DL #17: If you prepare to win, most times you will.

DL #18: Often there are hurdles to reaching your goals. If there is not a door, break through the wall and build on.

DL #19: To maximize potential you must minimize your social life. While it's great to have fun, success requires hustle.

DL #20: When that little voice inside your head is telling you "this is a bad idea," it is usually right. Sometimes small decisions can have a large impact. Don't forget: Decisions Determine Destiny.

DL #21: In tragic situations, leaders must show up. Exercise the "power of presence."

DL #22: Leaders should have personal goals outside of work and take affirmative steps to reach them.

DL 23: There are times when managers cannot rely on past victories. They must establish themselves as leaders in the present. This can be done only through decisive action.

DL #24: Turn your mistakes and failures into opportunities for success. Never give up! It's not over until you decide it's over.

DL #25: Pride comes before a fall. All managers should be able to admit when they're wrong. Some amount of vulnerability will lead to camaraderie with staff and other managers and will garner respect.

DL #26: Effective managers don't jump to conclusions without sufficient information.

DL #27: Remember: There will be some employees who hate the agency, and you're the company's poster child. They hate what you represent. Don't allow them to cause you to shirk your responsibilities.

DL #28: No shortcuts. Safety protocols exist for many reasons. A manager's number-one priority is to ensure that staff are safe. Review and practice.

DL #29: Effective leaders are adaptable and willing to do any job that is required for the team to succeed.

DL 30: Where ethics are concerned, an effective manager always does the right thing, regardless of the consequences,

DL #31: The harder we work for something, the more we appreciate it. Actually, the best lessons are often disguised as pain.

DL #32: The past doesn't have to determine the future. Many employees bring psychological scars into the workplace. It is vital that managers recognize these scars and help the employee to overcome them and build trust.

DL #33: When managers ask the right questions, in the right way, they are more likely to get the whole story.

DL#34: Emotional control is the foundation of great leadership. There will be situations every day that will push your psychological buttons, just because you're "right" doesn't make you "right".

DL #35: Employees don't care how much you know until they know how much your care. When an employee is experiencing difficulties, a quality manager always considers his or her wellbeing.

DL #36: Poor leaders can teach some great lessons. Keep a private journal on what not to do.

DL #37: Research the company and the interview panel, if possible, and prepare accordingly.

DL #38: When you allow yourself to develop a victim mindset you cease to progress. Master internal thoughts, or they will master you. Practice gratitude, focus on the positive side of life, and hold on.

DL #39: If you're a smart manager, don't look ignorant on paper. Work on the writing skills.

DL #40: Effective leaders realize they must put themselves out there to showcase their talents and gain influence. It's time to let your talents shine!

DL #41: A good leader gives his or her team members the permission and space to identify and use their talents, then fosters the development and celebration of these talents.

DL 42: Helping others is the highest form of fulfillment. Successful managers should always promote volunteer work.

DL#43: Reaching that next level requires sacrifice, organization, and discipline. Also, seek out a mentor. In due time, you'll become a mentor yourself.

DL #44: Never have too much pride to learn from your colleagues. A particular subject-matter expert or thought leader may be in your company or already on your team.

DL #45: Sometimes leaders have to dig deep inside to fulfill the mission. Dedication knows no bounds.

DL #46: The old adage, "Don't judge a book by its cover" can certainly ring true. Never underestimate your competitors' abilities to out-perform you. Keep your skills sharp.

DL#47: Effective managers will evolve and diversify their talents to move the needle forward in the agency.

DL #48: Don't be naive. Things may be going smoothly, but that can--and will--change at a moment's notice. Seal up as many cracks as possible with the right policies, procedures, and culture.

DL #49: Don't you dare be unprepared for that big opportunity! While no one should do things just to get promoted, there is nothing wrong with getting better at your job and pursuing career advancement.

DL #50: An interview is not the time to practice humility. In fact, it may be one of the few times to boast about your years of hard work and accomplishments.

DL #51: Avoid using "I" where possible. Any business, organization, or company is comprised of a team. You may be the quarter-back, but everyone plays an important role.

DL #52: If you're not organized, you're not in control.

DL #53: Never forget: Some employees are toddlers in adult bodies. Not only will managers supervise all types of people, they will be confronted with bizarre behavior and will have to de-cide when it becomes detrimental to the organization and take appropriate action.

DL #54: As a new leader, there is no grace period. Start establishing contacts, set your priorities, and don't get overwhelmed. You've got this!

DL #55: Effective leaders develop the skills necessary to thrive un-der pressure. For public speaking, practice, practice, practice. Use the mirror or speak to a small group of friends and fam-ily. Maybe your dog will listen!

DL #56: It's not where you come from but where you're heading that matters. Many times, we allow our background and surroundings to make us insecure. Never be intimidated by anyone. They're just mortals.

DL #57: Treat the janitor and the CEO the same. All human beings deserve dignity and respect.

DL #58: Some decisions may be outside of your expertise, but a decision must be made. Sometimes you have to trust your gut.

DL #59: Fear is the enemy and can only be defeated through strategies and practice. Keep chipping away at that wall.

DL #60: If you don't learn the art of delegation, you will constantly have monkeys on your back that don't belong to you.

DL #61: There are leaders who are decisive and use their past experiences and their gut to make decisions. While this may be effective, when possible, they should seek counsel, and review data to reach a positive outcome. If there is no time, roll on.

DL #62: There will be times when there won't be a consensus. Stop trying to please everyone and make a decision. Get acquainted with your gut. Hopefully, it will lead you in the right direction.

DL #63: Data is paramount in today's world of evidence-based outcomes. Nonetheless, as a manager, you have to be able to make quick decisions based on your experience. If the light is red, there's no time for data. Just stop the car.

DL #64: The highest standard is maintaining healthy staff and promoting a robust mission. When these align, other standards will be easy to implement.

DL #65: Unfortunately, there are managers who have poor standards and model behavior that is beneath their company's mission, and that behavior permeates throughout the organization. Leaders must set the tone.

DL #66: Managers must understand their roles and the roles of their staff, the proper chain of command, and the sufficient amount of information distributed to make sure time is not wasted.

DL #67: Effective communication is the backbone of any business. Without courage, communication will always be tainted.

DL #68: If you don't establish your role as a leader, someone else will fill the void and win the influence of staff. Establish credibility right out of the gate.

DL #69: Always pursue shared agreements and provide staff with clear expectations. Then expect the best but prepare for the worst.

DL #70 Climb off your high horse and mingle with your team. How long has it been since you met with line staff? There's no time like the present.

DL #71: Managers must make sure that staff at all levels know the company's vision, mission, and brand. They should also help solidify a nexus to their importance.

DL #72: Culture begins at the top and trickles down.

DL #73: Practice strategies and techniques to minimize fear through repetition.

DL #74: Good managers don't allow staff pedigree, education, or background to intimidate them. Instead, they embrace the authority vested in them and take the necessary steps to build confidence.

DL #75: Performance reviews should be an extension of ongoing, honest, and open dialogue between managers and employees, and should rarely produce any surprises.

DL #76: A proper feedback method will keep the meeting on track and expedite employee improvement.

DL#77: A reputable company must support employee actions as long as they are legal and within policy.

DL #78: A solid manager realizes that employees have different perspectives and backgrounds, but will find ways to leverage each group's gifts and talents and use those strengths to better the agency.

DL #79: Don't be intimidated or solely judge talent alone and choose the wrong person for a promotion. Instead, select the best candidate for the team and hold firm.

DL #80: In-person meetings, even when delivering bad news, are always the highest form of communication. Don't stress. Usually those who are disappointed will get over it in time.

DL #81: Some people will test your courage in dramatic fashion. Get ready now. Remember, whatever you permit, you promote.

DL #82: Some people just refuse to get along with their peers. In those cases, set boundaries. Manage people, not personalities.

DL #83: There is only one tribe. Either join or leave. As your organization grows, so will the derelicts. Deal with it.

DL #84: Don't allow manipulators to deafen your senses to opposing views. You need staff who will minimize your blind spots.

DL #85: Promotions will alter friendships. Accept it and handle them with a proactive strategy.

DL #86: In some organizations, middle managers are the pendulum of power. Middle managers should use their influence wisely and support one another and senior managers, if at all possible.

DL #87: Quality managers must embrace change to move the needle forward. If you're standing still while the rest of the world is moving forward, you might as well be walking backwards.

DL #88: Sometimes you have to use your head more than your heart. Decisions made from emotions alone will eventually hinder the mission and diminish respect for the leader.

DL #89: Don't discriminate or do special favors to give someone an advantage. When hiring staff, select the best candidate for the position. Take an objective look at talent, experience, motivation, education and values to make sure they fit the company's culture.

DL #90: Not only will a lack of confidentiality cause staff to lose trust for the manager, it might result in a personnel action.

DL #91: Managers will never gain respect when they model inappropriate behavior.

DL #92: When tempted, consider the long-term effects of your actions. Finding someone you trust to hold you accountable may be the extra encouragement you need to keep a barrier between your personal and professional life

DL #93: Not only does gossip harm others, it tarnishes the reputation and integrity of the gossiper. There are ways to get attention without hurting others.

DL #94: Good managers have a wellness plan that becomes habitual. It should include some form of diet, exercise, a fun hobby, and time with family and friends. These managers recognize that resilience is the key to true success.

DL #95: Never underestimate stress in the workplace. Management and staff wellness should be promoted in creative ways. The benefits are proven, and the overall health will create a higher level of production and minimize the need for sick leave. It may also save someone's life.

DL #96: Take time to find ways to get your team to experience the win when it happens. It's enjoyable. It's amazing for morale, service, and teamwork. It gets addictive.

DL #97: Give employees some individual victories, whether in-person or via video conference, phone calls or a hand-written note. It will go a long way.

DL #98: Always remind the team that setbacks are temporary, but a winning attitude is permanent.

DL #99: As soon as you can, head into the locker room at your company and get your team started on the path to victory.

DL #100: Leave it better than you found it!

ABOUT THE AUTHOR

 Ron is an author, speaker and founder and CEO of 4Ward Management Coaching.

Ron served as US Probation and Pretrial Services Safety and Training Division Chief and Academy Director at the Federal Law Enforcement Training Center in Charleston, South Carolina for eleven years. In that capacity, Ron oversaw new officer and advanced training, use of force policy, safety incident and search reporting and previously oversaw the US probation and pretrial services national wellness committee. Ron also served as Chair of the Federal Law Enforcement Training Accreditation Board of Directors for two years. He has over 30 years of law enforcement experience, beginning as a deputy sheriff and later becoming a state probation and parole officer and, finally, a U.S. Probation Officer, where he served for 14 years. Prior to being named Academy Director, Ron was a section chief and taught defensive tactics, along with several other courses, at the academy. He is a former AAU/USA East Coast Karate Silver Medalist. Ron holds a Bachelor of Arts degree in Education from Emory and Henry College, Emory, Virginia, and a Master of Science Degree in Criminal Justice Administration from Mountain State University, Beckley, West Virginia.

Made in USA - Kendallville, IN
86585_9781641117432
04.12.2023 1333